# Love
## vs.
# Anything
#### That Isn't

# LOVE
## vs.
# ANYTHING
## THAT ISN'T

How a Conscious Awareness of Love
Can Heal Us and Our World

D. SCOTT SONNENBURG

BALBOA
PRESS
A DIVISION OF HAY HOUSE

Copyright © 2013 D. Scott Sonnenburg.

All rights reserved. No part of this book may be used or reproduced by any means, graphic, electronic, or mechanical, including photocopying, recording, taping or by any information storage retrieval system without the written permission of the publisher except in the case of brief quotations embodied in critical articles and reviews.

Balboa Press books may be ordered through booksellers or by contacting:

Balboa Press
A Division of Hay House
1663 Liberty Drive
Bloomington, IN 47403
www.balboapress.com
1-(877) 407-4847

Because of the dynamic nature of the Internet, any web addresses or links contained in this book may have changed since publication and may no longer be valid. The views expressed in this work are solely those of the author and do not necessarily reflect the views of the publisher, and the publisher hereby disclaims any responsibility for them.

The author of this book does not dispense medical advice or prescribe the use of any technique as a form of treatment for physical, emotional, or medical problems without the advice of a physician, either directly or indirectly. The intent of the author is only to offer information of a general nature to help you in your quest for emotional and spiritual well-being. In the event you use any of the information in this book for yourself, which is your constitutional right, the author and the publisher assume no responsibility for your actions.

Certain stock imagery © Thinkstock.
Any people depicted in stock imagery provided by Thinkstock are models, and such images are being used for illustrative purposes only.

Printed in the United States of America

ISBN: 978-1-4525-6788-4 (e)
ISBN: 978-1-4525-6787-7 (sc)
ISBN: 978-1-4525-6789-1 (hc)

Library of Congress Control Number: 2013901907

Balboa Press rev. date: 2/20/2013

For Wanda,
without whom this work would not have seen the light of day.

And for my mom,
who passed away during the writing of this book.
Rest in peace. Thank you for the gift that is this life.

# Table of Contents

Preface  xi

Acknowledgments  xxi

Introduction  xxiii

### Chapter 1
**Open Eyes, Open Heart**  1

### Chapter 2
**Awakenings**  9

### Chapter 3
**The Death of My Companion**  21

### Chapter 4
**The Forest**  49

### Chapter 5
**Love**  51

### Chapter 6
**Fear**  59

### Chapter 7
**The Voice**  77

### Chapter 8
**Morning**  81

CHAPTER 9
Distraction   83

CHAPTER 10
Ego vs. Love   89

CHAPTER 11
Through God's Eyes   93

CHAPTER 12
Appreciation   95

CHAPTER 13
Love, Learning, and Loss   105

CHAPTER 14
The Endless Summer of the Heart   125

CHAPTER 15
Expectations and Suffering   131

CHAPTER 16
Morning Glory   139

CHAPTER 17
Chemical Craziness   143

CHAPTER 18
Passages   175

CHAPTER 19
Epilogue   181

"I was dead, then alive.
Weeping, then laughing.

The power of love came into me,
and I became fierce like a lion,
then tender like the evening star."
—Rumi

# Preface

Let's face it: humanity is a mess. And it is getting worse.

We are all too often a cruel, selfish, hurtful, and destructive species. Committing acts of barbarity against each other every minute of every day, we are wickedly quick to judge and condemn and agonizingly slow to understand and forgive. We seem to take a strange glee in categorizing, minimizing, and dehumanizing each other.

The headlines read like a horror story—innocent people killed for a few dollars or for being in the wrong place at the wrong time; children shot dead in the street for wearing the wrong clothes or for showing "disrespect" to another; and jilted lovers or disgruntled workers coolly walking into public places and methodically executing fellow human beings because they felt disrespected or minimized. How many times must we hear of someone's son, husband, or father beaten or shot dead because of an argument or traffic dispute?

On a larger scale, entire races, religions and governments are ever ready to annihilate each other—men, women, and children—because of religious intolerance, economic disagreement, or simple racial hatred. Children starve, while the adults running nation states invest billions upon billions of dollars to better arm themselves and find more efficient ways of killing each other.

We are heading down an unsustainable path of division politically, religiously, and morally. We seem to be running headlong into a fan blade of violence and chaos, a place of unbearable suffering and pain, all based on our unwillingness to see each other and our purpose clearly and in a higher way. The conflict present in our hearts and minds is being graphically reflected in the conflict seen throughout the world.

Throughout history, the story has been the same—only the characters and technology have changed. Most of human experience has been under the thumb of some form of tyranny. Whether religious, economic, or political, the results are the same: suffering, struggle, persecution, misery, and death.

But there is another form of tyranny, one that lies at the heart of it all—one that causes untold amounts of suffering. And this force exists inside us. In fact, most of us think it *is* us. It is the little voice that never quits talking; the critic that always has an opinion. This is the voice of chronic unrest and dissatisfaction, forever comparing, judging, and finding fault with ourselves and others. It is the voice that keeps us always searching, always protecting, always wanting more, and never really knowing why. It is the inner judge that never takes a break, forever telling us we are not good enough, smart enough, thin enough, or rich enough. This is the inner whisper of doubt and fear that colors most of human experience, keeping us from peace, both within the privacy of our own hearts and our civilization as a whole.

This is the voice of separation and fear that creates and tolerates violence and war; it is the force that condones bondage and hatred of all kinds as forms of protection and even justice. It is the voice that says it is okay to hurt, maim, or kill to get what is needed, to protect what has already been gotten, or to enforce an idea or opinion that is seen to be the only right one.

Since nothing can manifest externally which is not first conceived and nurtured internally, this toxic inner conversation, seemingly private and harmless, is the causative agent behind the chaotic and painful world we see.

The pain and confusion of living disconnected from what sustains us, and the fear resulting from the perceived separation from the organizing, creative, and loving force, which most call God, is the reason for the misery from which humanity currently suffers. In many cases, the pain of separation induced by judgment is seemingly innocuous. But the violence inflicted by looking in the mirror and hating what you see is of the same origin as what creates depression, addiction, and disease. The violence inflicted, whether in thought or action, on your brother when he does something as simple as cut you off in traffic, is of the same character as what causes war. It is a simply a matter of degree.

Most of humanity is numb and disconnected from life's source, and the resulting pain and misery are palpable on a global scale. The suffering inherent within our perceived separation and isolation from what created and sustains us is reflected in abject poverty, famine, and war. And with the advent of modern weaponry, this spiritual wounding threatens all life on earth.

As a planet, we are headed for a fall. Storm clouds are gathering, fed by an accumulation of religious intolerance, greed, and a profound ignorance of what truly sustains us. As one soul, we are wounded.

Our collective pain, dysfunction, and disharmony is growing; life seems to be getting harder, less fluid, and more contentious personally, societally, and geopolitically. The tension currently building is analogous to that of a bow being slowly drawn. The energy is gathering, and soon it will be inevitably and devastatingly released. This is felt by most people but not well examined, processed, or understood.

Since September 11, 2001, humanity has become more fearful, more animalistic, and more cynical while becoming less loving, less tolerant, and less secure; life changed that day in many subtle and not subtle ways. We put on a happy face and go about our days, embracing distraction, mostly because we feel we cannot do anything else. But deep inside, an empty gnawing is ever present, a friction, a constant and fatiguing internal diligence guarding against things unseen and unknown. It is dark within that roiling discomfort deep inside, in that mysterious place which lies beyond words.

A potent mix of anger, frustration, and mistrust lies under the surface of most of our lives; it begs for acknowledgment and reconciliation but receives none. We doubt, fear, and hide, not trusting anybody or anything except for those closest to us, and even this requires a level of vulnerability we are not comfortable with. So walls are built to keep our enemies out and to protect what precious little we may have. And to protect it, we will kill or die.

We call ourselves civilized and elevate ourselves above the animals while at the same time perpetrating and accepting barbarism on a global scale that would have most "lower" creatures shaking their heads at the insanity, if they could even believe it. And it is within our most "civilized" creations—our cities—where the most heartless and disturbing acts of depravity routinely take place.

Humans have an amazing propensity to complicate things, to overly study, quantify, and categorize, while at the same time completely missing the big picture. We whistle while walking past the graveyard, looking the other way, hoping the violence with which we are surrounded won't affect us or our loved ones. But inevitably, it will.

In fact, it already has.

As a society, we are wounded by our collective insanity. We try to deny the horror while speaking in hushed voices behind iron gates and locked doors. We will do anything but look directly at the train wreck that is the evening news. After all, bad things happen to *them*, not us. But the wound of the mother whose child was taken by gang violence is our wound. The wound created by the kidnapping, rape, and murder of a little girl is our wound. The wounds at the heart of homelessness, racism, addiction, terrorism, and domestic violence are *our wounds*.

In an ongoing and whirling flourish of unmitigated madness, we nurture, tend to, and feed our wounds, thus creating more wounds. The question is this: how do we break the cycle and truly heal?

To be healed is to be made whole again; to be made whole again is to heal the chasm separating us from ourselves and each other, thereby reconnecting to all that is. We go to great lengths to separate ourselves from each other, nature, and our Source, and it is within this separation we suffer. We, as a matter of routine, trash and disrespect our gifts, our environment, our hearts, our bodies, and each other. We are better than this. We are higher than this. We must remember we are *one* in every sense of the word. There is no judgment other than our own, and there is no separation other than that we insinuate into our experience willingly. Our suffering is *always* created by us globally, locally or personally. It is always our choice.

Fear is endemic in this world, deeply ingrained in the institutions of politics, religion, science, and medicine. How can we expect to be sane when the guiding and regulating "pillars" of modern civilization are themselves insane? Remove fear, and these bloated entities would collapse under their own weight.

Fear is born of the ignorance of our true nature and our essence as well as the resulting denial of the infinite and loving nature deep within us all. We are of God, not separate from it, so how can we be so fearful, ugly, small, petty, and vindictive? Is that which we call God fearful, ugly, small, petty, and vindictive?

What we know as ego is where the separation lies. It is within its perverted sense of survival at any cost where pain is born and thrives. When the selfish and oppositional nature of the ego, reflective in statements like "This is mine; that is yours," "I am this, and you are that," and "I am right, so you must be wrong," is lived and accepted as truth, misery ensues. It is almost comical that our deepest and most painful issues are caused by something as simple as drawing a line in the sand.

Combine the primal thought process of ego with the intellect of the human species, and a recipe for disaster results. Combine self-righteousness, unrestrained self-interest, and fervent religiosity with intellect sufficient to create nuclear weapons, and life on this planet can be forever altered.

It should be no surprise that when the idea of God is misconstrued and perverted by the egoic[1], selfish, and fearful, the result is devastation and suffering. Similarly, when the power of the atom, which powers all life on this planet in the form of sunlight, is misconstrued and perverted by the egoic, selfish, and fearful, the specter of hell on earth is raised. Unfortunately, the marriage of these ideas likely assures it.

From world wars to sleepless nights, the ego is responsible for untold amounts of human suffering, and the collective ego of humanity seems to be ready and willing to take us all down a very ugly path.

What we witness as evil is simply the result of the disallowance of the connection to and the inner knowledge of what we call God. The brutality, the utterly mindless barbarity, is born in the darkness of illusion; it cannot exist within the light

---

1  Arising from the ego; a state where one is identified with the ego and the idea of the separate self.

of truth. True knowledge is the way out of the madness, not the fear-based knowledge predicated upon opinion, judgment, separation, exclusion, and control that passes for knowledge so often.

What we know of as hell is of our own creation, and we dwell within its prison of pain and suffering willingly. Much effort is expended creating and maintaining our own personalized hells: incessant discrimination, endless judgment, and self-condemnation manifested by chronic dissatisfaction, joylessness, and hyper-vigilance, all stemming from runaway thought. All will result inevitably in illness, addiction, depression, and anxiety. From these personal hells are born the hells of society: crime, poverty, violence, racism, and religious persecution. From society's hells are born the collective hells of the human race responsible for endless mass suffering and the wanton destruction of each other and the planet itself.

These hells are entirely man-made; they are not of God. They are not punishments; they are merely cause and effect. They are the result of forgetting who and what we are, and they can be erased within the clarity of a single moment of unfettered awareness, an experience that seems so rare yet is ever available. Heaven is *always* ours and is as close as our next breath.

What we desire most is what we know but have forgotten. Unconsciously, we feel a primal pull toward the higher parts of ourselves, to the essence of the divine, the loving spark of creation dwelling within every molecule of our being. It is at once impossibly close and so far away. The joy of life is realized as we awaken to the truth one by one—sometimes over a lifetime, sometimes in a flash—until collectively we rise out of the ashes of what was once thought to be real but was revealed to be nothing but a painful fantasy.

All healing occurs within. Peaceful people make for peaceful communities, which make for peaceful countries, which may even lead to a peaceful world, if one can imagine such a thing. The power of one person connected to Source and living in a state of radiant and loving bliss can change the world. The power of such a person is exponentially more impactful than any politician or world leader could hope to be, unless they themselves are connected in such a way, a seemingly rare occurrence. Every loving thought makes the world better, and every thought of separation does not. It is a battle. It could be said this is the ultimate battle of good vs. evil, dark vs. light, ego vs. heart, right vs. wrong, God vs. the Devil, or whatever symbolism appeals to you. I think of it as the battle of *Love vs. Anything That Isn't*.

But even that isn't entirely accurate. There is no opposite of the blinding and complete Love from which we all arise and will soon return. All separation is illusion. But that doesn't mean the illusion can't make us miserable. It surely does within the framework of this world. Our job is to realize the split within ourselves and to locate and repair the fractures within our hearts, within our very being. By so doing, using Love as the tool, the fractures within our collective soul will be repaired as well. Only then will we return to our rightful place in the light.

# Acknowledgments

I would like to thank first the craniosacral therapists who have treated me and with whom I have learned, taught, and worked. Without you, none of this would have been possible: Kelly Chick PT, CST; Stan Gerome LMT, CST-D; Michael Morgan LMT, CST; and Dr. John Upledger. There are many others who have taught me many things in many classes but I cannot remember all your names, but I do remember all of you.

I want to thank all the clients I have been so privileged to know and treat. You have each taught me things in many unforgettable and amazing ways.

I want to thank my good friends who have supported and encouraged me to write even when my ego told me I had nothing that was worth sharing: Kristin Lloyd-Heaton LPC, M.Ed.; Sherald Najera; Kari Uselman PhD; Patrice Artress RN, PhD; and Tina Curtis PT.

I want to thank my family for simply being my family, especially my brothers, Steve, James and Joe.

I wish to extend gratitude to my mother and father. Together you gave me the gift of a good start with a blank canvas so that I might paint the beautiful picture that has become my life.

# Introduction

This is a book about discovery. It is a book about darkness and light, but most of all, it is a book of remembering.

God and Love are two things I didn't contemplate much for most of my life. It wasn't that I didn't ponder the great mysteries ... I frequently wondered what life was all about. I read much and was fairly educated in the scientific opinion of reality, but it always seemed to be a nebulous pursuit. I took comfort in rationality and the fact I was intellectually capable of comprehending what the academics were teaching, but I never got past the feeling there was one heck of an elephant hiding somewhere in the room.

I was not and still don't consider myself religious in the conventional sense. I am thankful I wasn't raised in a religious home. This allowed me to form my own ideas, even if those ideas (which I more accurately know now as knowingness arising from the heart rather than the intellect) came from years of suffering, making mistakes, and generally getting things wrong.

Even as a child, traditional religion didn't resonate with me. The stories didn't make sense, and the overall feeling I got from it was disconcerting and a bit uncomfortable. Something didn't seem right. It didn't seem genuine. It just didn't seem real.

So I rebelled in what seemed the only way possible for someone who didn't believe in religion. I called myself an atheist.

I was and still am of the thought that it is not necessary to be religious in the classic sense to be a good person, if goodness is defined by kindness, generosity, and love. I am frustrated by those who profess theirs is the only way, that only those who feel and act as they do can possibly be good or righteous, valuable or smart. This applies to the scientific rationalists/atheists as well as believers, as both groups seem equally eager to separate, judge, and minimize those with differing views.

I always knew intuitively that if there was a God, he surely wouldn't be so small or petty to choose just a few of his children—only those who believed in him in a specific way—to go to heaven or garner his Love. I knew if he bothered to create something as magnificent as a butterfly or a human being, his Love must extend equally and always. In my heart, I knew these things, and as I wandered aimlessly through my life I often thought of them, but I continued to call myself an atheist almost as a defense against the onslaught of the raucous and intolerant religious tone all around me.

But I was never comfortable with the term *atheist*, so I vacillated between that and another completely erroneous label: *agnostic*. And like most people of these belief systems, I trusted science. But the more I heard from the highly educated and so-called "rational," the more it left me cold as well. It couldn't tell me how I can be moved to tears by a beautiful piece of music; it couldn't explain emotions, consciousness, or the *reason* I am alive and here. It could perhaps attempt to describe how I thought, but it couldn't tell me *why* I thought.

My common sense and intuition had issues here as well. A purely random view of existence is that through the vagaries of chance, all the constituent chemicals necessary for life came together over an immense amount of time and formed you and me, as well as the immense number of living things that have existed on this planet over countless millennia. It maintains that DNA itself is an accident, as is our immune system, our heartbeat, and our sense of joy. Is the smile brought on by hearing the laughter of a child the result of a random series of events without reason or purpose?

We are very good at describing life in a mechanical sense. We can categorize, theorize, and quantify many aspects of what we know and describe as life, but we cannot explain with any sense of universal accuracy what it means to actually be alive. Science cannot explain how consciousness can emanate from matter or from where it comes at all. It cannot explain how and why I am aware of myself as I write these words, as aware as you are right now reading them.

Everything we touch, see, feel, and physically are emerged billions of years ago in a furnace in the heart of a star. How could this random assortment of molecules and atoms, lifeless compounds—star stuff—assemble itself into what I know as a horse, a starfish, or me? There seems to be quite a gap between raw, inanimate matter and the animated, thinking, feeling miracle of life, yet there is no scientific definition as such to describe it.

The purely nuts-and-bolts view of things always struck me as lacking imagination. Gazing at the stars, I would wonder. *There must surely be more to life than this. What is the purpose? Where is the reason?* Without a preformed and preinstalled opinion of creation, religious or otherwise, to color my perception, I knew the stars must have a reason beyond simply decorating the night sky and beyond the cold, scientific description of their chemistry and physics. I knew the song of the wind in the leaves hinting at the memories of those I've loved and lost must have a reason as well. But, if I entertain the notion these things don't have a reason, does the way they make me feel have one? Does anything become more alive, pertinent, or valuable if understood scientifically? Does the reason for all this wonder and beauty live in tables and graphs, equations and taxonomic classification?

For so long, I walked the line between the believers and the rationalists, and in many cases still do. I found myself wandering and watching, listening to them shout at each other, stuck between those having blind faith and those who required proof for everything. Walking the line between superstition and skepticism, I dwelled in no-man's-land somewhere between heart and mind. Or more accurately, perhaps I dwelled in the strange place where they meet.

I believe many people find themselves here. We are complex bundles of flesh and memory, motivated by divergent things, each having a unique experience, each imbued with unique perspective, sharing this one world. There are many who feel they walk somewhere in the middle of the hard definitions put upon us by ourselves, and others who seem so sure of what is good, right, necessary, or *real*. Neither conservative nor liberal, neither religious nor atheist, and neither unduly skeptical nor superstitious, there are those of us who simply feel we don't know what life is all about, and we are okay with that. We know there is merit to science performed within a given context to improve human life and protect the environment, and there is equal merit to being open to the fact there is much more to life than science could ever hope to explain. There is merit in having humility, in realizing science is limited in its scope and subject to bias, and in realizing life will always be much bigger than our ability to describe it. There is freedom, and even a sense of relief, within the acceptance of the fact that no matter how hard we try, we can't quantify, categorize, and explain all natural phenomena inclusive of the life experience and what we call "God."

After some life-changing personal experiences, I suddenly became aware of the fact there is much more to life than I previously had thought. After suffering chronic pain for over twenty years, I came upon something called craniosacral therapy (CST), and it changed my life forever.

One day in March 2007, after several weeks of the therapy during which my pain was totally eradicated, I had a very powerful spiritual experience that changed everything about me and the way I look at life. I came out of that experience with a level of awareness I never had known was possible. I'd suddenly been given the gift of profound peace, along with a deep sense of comfort and awareness, which has never left me. I feel what happened that day was akin to a near-death experience in the effect it had on my way of living and my way of being. I left the treatment room on a bright and cool spring day, knowing there was so much more to me and to life than I ever could have imagined.

I'd entered the clinic an atheist and left a deeply and profoundly spiritual man. I encountered something that put my intellect, ego, and inner judge in its place. I realize now it was not that I didn't believe in God; it was that I didn't believe in *religion*. To me, there can be quite a distinction between the two, which is itself a massive subject. This book will touch on what most people call God quite often, because it is an awareness of divine Source that pervades everything I am and do, every heartbeat, and every breath. Of course, this is present within each of us. It is the remembering of this essential fact that transforms everything to its rightful and natural place; it begets an effortless and beautiful state of being.

Ralph Waldo Emerson wrote, "God enters by a private door into every individual." I am not of the thinking there is only one way to realize God, nor do I believe we are here to express God in a homogenous way. And I believe that is what we are here to do—express God by simply being what God is—Love. It's really very simple, but as we so often do, we have overcomplicated the issue and institutionalized and ritualized the concept of God. We have made the celebration of God cumbersome and often rigid. By so doing, we have made divine knowledge seem somehow exclusive, hard to attain, available only to those who play by a predetermined set of rules. I, by necessity more than design, choose to defy religious categorization. I am human, and that is the only categorization I will accept. My experience is unique, my knowledge is unique, and my perception of my Source is unique. I do not adhere to any particular religion or spiritual practice and do not espouse any either. I tend to think of my creator in much less specific and much larger ways. What I know as God is not a "him." It is really more an "it," for lack of a better term. What I know as God is expressed as unlimited Love, pure and simple. Not the love syrupy songs are written about but the blinding, perfect, radiant, shining, luminous, and endless Love at the heart of all creation.

Through all the confusion created by living in a society that is profoundly confused, we seem to have forgotten we are born for reason—a higher and more beautiful one than most will ever know in this life. What keeps us from knowing this and from embracing our inner beauty?

We try hard to remain ignorant of what really matters, taking ourselves seriously in regards to things which matter not and not taking ourselves seriously enough in many ways we should. We continually mistake illusion for reality, bad for good, dark for light, and possession for Love. And for these reasons and many more, we are miserable.

What causes us to fear and avoid our very center, that which is essential and which is the real us? What causes us to run and hide from our brilliance? What causes us to be content with passing the days, asleep and disconnected, focused on the menial tasks at hand, simply trying to get through the day, only to get up and do it all over again tomorrow?

What do we see when all is quiet and we look in the mirror? Do we see the Love and light, or do we see something needing work, something not good enough? Do we see what lies behind our eyes or just the bags beneath them? Do we see something in need of repair, something that is broken, something somehow less than what we think ourselves should be? Look closely. Can you see the pain in your own eyes? Can you see the child?

In a world that is becoming more and more disconnected, divided, heartless, and cruel, I want this book to simply serve as a reminder of our brilliance beyond any appearance or illusion, a reminder of our inherent beauty and goodness. It is time to embrace the angel within; it is time to reconnect to our lifeline; it is time to come home to ourselves and our peace. It is time to awaken from the nightmare that defines so much of human experience and live in ways more consistent with our Source and essential nature.

I write this to express myself and relate what I have learned as much as to simply share with others my joy. This book was inevitable once I caught a glimpse of the light, even though it took several years to actually put together. It is not meant to change minds or opinions as much as to relate to others the experience of one life lived via the heart. It is based on my personal experience. All that follows was intuitively received and is intellectually given with the hope that the essence of the deeper and more ethereal levels from which the knowledge arises is communicated with any sense of accuracy. The subjects covered in this book are by definition somewhat obscure when held in contrast with common, everyday experience, and they can be frustratingly difficult to communicate with mere words. All words can do is point to the truth, which is always experiential and will always lie somewhere beyond them.

There are many paths to paradise, and it is apparent that a spiritual revolution is already underway. My place, I feel, is to simply describe the miraculous nature of my transition from a depressed and hopeless soul who possessed little faith in anything—a wounded spirit who had given up on himself and humanity—to someone who lives every moment with a profound sense of peace, gratitude, purpose and Love. If I can do it, anyone can. I am not by any means special.

Craniosacral therapy, for reasons mostly intuited and others yet to be discovered, showed me the way back to myself. It helped remove tons of rock to uncover the shining diamond of my true being buried deep within. I believe every human on earth has this same sparkling essence buried somewhere. It is waiting to be uncovered. Every human has a right to know it.

This is simply my story, a personal account of how I realized an enduring sense of inner peace, which so far has been able to withstand all storms. I have been *reminded* of my beauty and the beauty of all life. And we are beautiful, all of us, by the very fact of our creation. We are sourced from unmitigated Love and beauty, though some people act in ways not so loving and not so beautiful. How do we reconcile the fact that we are simultaneously capable of such amazing feats of loving creation and such dark acts of destruction and hatred? How is it we can create a symphony or a space shuttle one moment and beat each other to death over a difference of opinion the next?

What I have remembered and will share with you is that we are essentially good, but are in training, so to speak. The outer parts of us, the roles we play in this physical realm responsible for our deeds and actions, are often not in line with the higher truths—*our* higher truths. The evidence is incontrovertible and everywhere. Ours is currently a world defined by suffering and hatred; it is a world rife with violence, disease, and pain. It would seem we are lost. But the good news is we can always be found. We do this by rediscovering that part of us which was never lost and never could be—that formless and eternal loving witness of all you are and have ever been—a part of you that is always present, always perfect, and always waiting.

The human race in its present incarnation has nearly run its course and will destroy itself and the planet if a fundamental paradigm shift does not occur. I do not believe this is the destiny of humanity. As we spin into the most dangerous and potentially violent time in our history, as we fall farther into the madness, there are many who find themselves rising above it. It is as if the darker the world gets, the more some are, by necessity, quietly radiating more and more Love and light. The new human who is capable of recognizing what its purpose really is (to know Love), what its true nature is (to be Love), and what it is here for (to learn how to love completely and unconditionally) is the only hope for the survival of the species.

We learn by suffering, by getting things wrong—or we don't. The lesson is simple: there is Love and nothing else. And at our current level of development, we learn what Love truly is by experiencing all the horrors of what it isn't.

We are little shards of divine light having a physical experience for the reasons of growth and expansion and ultimately to get closer to what created us. We are very good at skirting the edges of what we really are, never fully immersing ourselves into our own essence, the places where we truly live. It is time to come home.

The simple and grand truth is we are divine and perfect in essence although fractured and broken on the surface. We are angels. We just don't know it yet.

# Chapter 1

## Open Eyes, Open Heart

The cool air kissed my warm, moist skin as I crested yet another hill, creating a pleasant menthol-like contrast that was cool and refreshing.

Heart pounding and lungs burning I hiked through the woods, attention focused at the terrain beneath my feet, happily lost and held trancelike by the rhythmic crunch. Following a fast-moving whitewater creek, I walked quickly and smoothly, feeling the power in my legs build with every step, marveling at how the myriad muscles, tendons, and ligaments contracted and relaxed, pushed and pulled, and worked in perfect synchronous relation to give me motion.

Gliding through the trees, I soon became aware of a strange yet pleasant feeling as the sound of the gravel's crunch beneath my feet slowly began to fade. Soon I realized I could no longer feel the ground in any solid way. Aware of my breathing, I no longer felt it physically; it seemed as if it were happening somewhere beyond—close yet far away. Sensing my heart's rhythm, I was strangely disconnected from it; it was mine, yet it wasn't. At once, I was deeply aware of everything yet strangely disconnected from it all.

It was spring in southeast Alaska. I was feeling very alive, and like the land, I was in the midst of an awakening. In this predominantly gray and rainy world, this day was a rarity: cloudless, sunny, and crisp. Drinking in the blue above, I walked through the coastal rainforest while trying to shrug off another long, dark, and cold winter.

Stubborn patches of snow hid in the shadows, but the remainder of the forest was green and soggy, save for the gravel trail. I'd walked this path many times, and as always when immersed in such an environment, I was deeply happy. There to exercise my body, touch nature, and simply be quiet in a world which is so rarely so, I had every reason to believe I was alone. But miles from the trailhead on a sparsely inhabited island, completely alone, in the middle of the largest temperate rainforest on earth, one can truly hear things—and not always with one's ears.

The trail was a roller coaster with numerous ups and downs, forever winding. The sound of water was constant. The distant roar of numerous waterfalls echoing against the nearby mountainside, along with the bubbling of countless small creeks imbued the forest with a hypnotic soundtrack, lending a sense of living motion. On this bright day, the shadows of the towering Sitka spruce and red cedar sharply framed the brilliant green open patches of moss, lichen, and ferns. In the penumbra, boughs waving in the breeze fractured the light into a kaleidoscopic array shimmering on the forest floor.

Continuing on, moving without any sense of effort, I soon neared the high point on the trail where I came out of the trees and into the light.

It turns out this was true in more ways than one.

I was suddenly compelled to stop. Surrounded by fallen trees covered in moss, weak sunlight on my skin, I breathed deeply, watching my exhalations turn to vapor, drops of sweat running down my forehead. As I caught my breath, I began to feel as if I was being watched.

Somewhat unsettled, I turned and looked into the dark forest from which I had just emerged, and I saw nothing. I then looked to the nearby mountaintops expecting—but not exactly wanting—to see eyes looking back at me. My gaze returned nothing but green stillness.

Then subtly, almost imperceptibly, from nowhere and everywhere, a faint buzz, like that of a swarm of flying insects but much more subtle—more round, fuzzy, and sweet—oozed from out of the ether. As the sound swirled, danced, and then enveloped me, I came to realize it was not my ears with which I was hearing this— it was my entire body.

I stood there amazed, as whatever this was seemed to penetrate every bit of me. I was completely without fear. On a deep level, I knew I was in the best of hands.

The buzzing continued as I stood still and watched. Slowly fading into a state of blissful detachment—from my body, thoughts, and environment—I was soon completely overwhelmed by a feeling so sweet and delicate, so perfect, so profoundly gentle and loving, so … *peaceful*. The pain and struggle of being human seemed a distant dream.

My senses dulled, as if they needed to be turned down in order to hear what I was hearing, sense what I was sensing, and feel what I was feeling. I felt as if I had been submerged in a deep, warm, and loving pool. The sound intensified and diminished, swelled and retreated, seeming to react intelligently to the attention I was giving it, eventually filling every bit of my awareness as it crossed from the external environment through my physical body to the depths of my soul. I never wanted it to end.

Soon the realization was made this was not a sound at all; it was something different, something new, something *more*. It wasn't physical, and I was not perceiving it physically. This was occurring on a much deeper level, a level for which I have no words, for which there are no words.

Now completely immersed in this sensation, I realized what I was "hearing" was the sound of life itself—the buzzing was the sound of my cells humming with the business of life! I was hearing without ears and seeing without eyes their workings, and there they were, shimmering like ice crystals floating in the sunlight; I saw their light, their machinery, their intelligence, their *life*. I saw how their symphony was giving life to the song which was me. A knowing fell upon my heart. Each cell was aware. Each and every one was conscious and alive and able to feel everything I felt. Each was intelligent and independent, yet all were *me*. Somehow, they let me know that like us as individual humans, each cell is a drop in a greater ocean, independent yet coherent and necessary within the greater whole—each with a reason to be.

Stunned and filled with awe, I reveled in what I was witnessing. For whatever reason, life was showing me something special, and I was deeply moved and profoundly humbled.

I fell to my knees and then found myself sitting cross-legged on the cold gravel. I sat and gazed at the surrounding wilderness with eyes full of childlike wonder when suddenly the world expanded.

I could hear the trees.

There were now billions of loving eyes upon me, and although by myself, I've never been less alone. I was aware of all life on a deep and sacred level. And even better and more amazing, *it was aware of me*. Sensing I was in the presence of a countless number of loving beings, it felt as if I were being warmly welcomed back after a long time away. An infinite number of glistening points of light swirled within and all around me, and a mutual exchange of perfect, effortless Love was occurring among them all. A veil had been lifted, and the entire world was utterly and indescribably beautiful and alive. It was such an epic feeling of connection, of belonging and peace; it was immensely moving. And ... it was familiar. I knew this was a homecoming. This was who I am, and this was where I came from.

Impossibly alive, comforted, and blissful, feeling connected beyond description, the immensity and glory of what continued to pervade the deepest depths of my being that afternoon greatly exceeds my ability to describe with words, so I will not attempt to do so any further. I am as humbled and moved by it now as when it occurred.

Through this life-redefining experience, a message was clearly and lovingly given: there really is more.

What was shown to me was that there is much more to us than we can imagine. There is so much we don't know, and much of what we think we do know and what we think is important is at the very least superficial, if not completely irrelevant. I was shown there is infinitely more to the world and to life than science or the rational mind can describe or ever hope to understand. There is more to us and the reasons for our lives, the reasons for our being, the reasons for our existence than we are ever taught by society, religion, or science. We are so very much more than we are ever encouraged or even allowed to think.

It was given to me that the world in which we live, this seemingly concrete "reality," is but a fraction, a snapshot—an infinitesimal sliver—of a larger, much more essential reality. And the tools necessary for comprehending its greater truths are inherent yet dormant within most of us.

Indelibly imbued into my heart that day was the knowing we are protected and loved more than we can imagine. And make no mistake: we are as eternal as the stars. But we are mostly ignorant of these higher truths, *choosing* instead to live within the illusion of limitation and lack, of separation and fear, and of struggle, darkness, and death.

The truth is there is perfect beauty happening within every living thing; and dwelling within every moment, there is more

Love than could ever be intellectually known. All of life is purposeful, and it is all divine.

The most miraculous gift given me that day by the billion points of light was the inner knowing there is nothing to fear in this life. We are not vulnerable in any way. Death is nothing but an illusion. Death is nothing but a return.

We are part of the most beautiful and glorious of dances, and our gifts are many. We are alive, we *are* Love, and we are spinning together through the immensity of creation on this magnificent rock, embraced and held within a caring, intelligent, and loving Universe. This is all we should need to be happy and fulfilled. Why is it so difficult for us to simply rest in this fact? Why do we struggle and suffer? Why do we fight and judge, brutalize and kill?

Held within every moment, the glory of creation is displayed for us in impossibly profound and everlasting beauty. Everywhere we look, it is ours to behold and make part of our experience. Our beauty and the beauty of all life are right in front of us always. Yet through errors of perception that we are taught and for the most part continue to embrace, we continue to remain blind to these most essential and obvious gifts.

I left the woods wanting to say to my fellow man, "Look at your life, look at the wonder, and look at the beauty. What is it going to take to get you to see the grace inherent within you? What is it going to take to get you to see that the essence of what created you is within you always? You are inseparable from that beauty. You are an important and essential part of all that is, was, and will ever be; you are divine Love expressing itself through the act of being human, through the act of living, and through the act of *loving*. Let the stars' gentle flicker at night remind you, as well as the immutable power of the tide—their immensity is your immensity; their timelessness is your timelessness.

What I was left with that day is the knowledge that what is needed is an increase in everyday awareness to include the fact all life is a wondrous and sacred miracle emanating entirely from the force we call Love or God, to me those words are indistinguishable. The animating forces of life—the higher, deeper, and more essential realms, which give rise to all that is—are universally loving and ever present. There is no such thing as being alone. There are connections between each of us and all of life, from every cell within every living thing to each and every leaf on every tree. From the depths of the ocean to the farthest reaches of this and every galaxy, there is an infinitely and incomprehensibly grand web of interrelationship, which does more than hint at the underlying truth of the unity of all life.

The buzzing eventually faded out of perception and the forest was again quiet. Stunned, moved, and crying with happiness I had never known, I sat on the trail as the afternoon's shadows approached and I began to become chilled. I don't know how much time passed as my tears crossed my smile to fall upon the earth. Fuzzy, weak, and profoundly changed, I got up and slowly walked back to the car.

## Chapter 2

## *Awakenings*

The experience in the Alaska woods was one of several I had in early 2007. The combined effect of all of them was to change me from a man who didn't give much attention to what couldn't be quantified, measured, or proven to a man who walks every step of his life with a deep awareness that what is not seen is immeasurably more important and essential than anything that is.

It took over forty years of suffering and wandering aimlessly through life to figure this out, but this doesn't make me unusual. I, like most, had bought into the version of reality forced upon us by society from a very early age, a version that has little if anything to do with truth, peace, or genuine fulfillment.

My entire life, I didn't give this much thought. I lived as I was told by my family, government, teachers, and society. I was an unconscious cog in the machine. I didn't think I was that unhappy, but then what could I know about true happiness? I thought the material world with which I was surrounded was all there was.

I was a good and proud American, a decent human being, a nice guy; I never hurt anybody—not directly or intentionally anyway. I didn't believe in God or in anything I couldn't see; nature and even my own existence could be broken down into provable theories and formulas that were reproducible in a lab. Everything always had a logical explanation. It had to, or how could it possibly exist? I considered myself a reasonable and logical man, a critical thinker, and I was proud to call myself a skeptic. Comfortable in my intellect, I took refuge in my rational nature, but in reality, I was too lost in my own thinking to know how lost I really was.

I was asleep, unconscious, and on autopilot, investing in so much that wasn't necessary and believing so much that wasn't true. A slave to my opinions, I was completely and utterly disconnected from any and all awareness of the larger picture. In other words, I was like most everyone else.

For many years, I lived a comfortable, albeit painful, life. I worked hard and partied and tried to have fun, because I knew nothing else. My not uncommon version of reality was that you're born, go to school, get a job, work, retire, and then die. And that's about it.

So I did all the things a good American must do to be happy: work hard, contribute to a 401(k), vote in every election, buy lots of useless stuff, and go to great lengths to stay busy. I did all this, all the things society told me I needed to do, in order to fit in and be responsible. And through ever mounting pain and a stifling apathy, I kept at it, but never with a clear sense in my heart as to why.

I got up in the morning because I had to, not because I wanted to, and I passed my days mindlessly, turning the pages of my life's story without really reading them. Impatient and always wanting to skip ahead to the next chapter, hoping to see if this tale would get any more *interesting*, I lived according to the way countless strangers told me to live. I thought the way they told me to think, and I did what they told me to do. And I suffered and struggled because somewhere inside I knew it was all wrong.

I stayed willingly numb and played the game, hiding in plain sight from myself and everyone I knew because that's what's expected and accepted in this society as *normal*. Playing a role I didn't particularly want to play but not knowing how to change it, I embraced the lies—not just about what I am and need to be, but more importantly about *what I am not* and could never be.

The voices came from all directions with their opinions and judgments, but by far the most powerful one was my own. The conversation in my head was overwhelming and never ending. Forever criticizing, judging, quantifying, and discerning, putting things into little boxes to be stored away, the voices slowly grew from whispers to shouts.

The following is something I wrote some time before I opened my eyes. I can vividly remember the tortured and confused man who wrote it, and it strikes me as a good marker for who and what I was at the time.

It's very painful really, thinking about the past, trying to pinpoint exactly where I went wrong. It is necessary, I know, but attempting to penetrate the defenses, the armor, the layer of emotional skin which covers and protects our most precious, delicate, and elemental being is dangerous business. There can be some scary things in there. I have to do it though; I have to figure some things out … for self-preservation.

I am living in such profound emotional and physical pain it's nearly unbearable. So like a surgeon and his knife, I must cut deeply and precisely. I must remove the bad tissue and leave as much of the good as possible. But like any incision that runs deep, it will hurt, and it will surely leave a scar.

I've been having a conversation with myself—more of an argument really. Every day I ask questions, make statements, yell, scream, and sometimes (though very rarely) laugh. Sometimes, I feel as if this show going on between my ears needs a soundtrack because it's like a bad movie … without the hideously overpriced popcorn.

You see, I'm a broken man. Mentally and physically damaged, I am in constant physical pain, and simply put, I'm miserable. While every day I have flashes of what life could be or should be and I actually get excited about it, the feelings are always frustratingly evanescent. Some physical pain or sudden memory of a stupid mistake from the past will serve to destroy any hope I have of feeling alive again. I am amazed at how effective these things are at distracting me and keeping me from my peace—peace I know is mine. I just don't know where I left it. Inevitably, the train carrying any glimmer of inspiration or happiness will derail and crash and burn, again with no survivors.

It seems this universe, the one between my ears, while exceedingly close and intimate, is at once (at least in my case, the only one of which I can be sure) so foreign, so strange, so unreachable, and so mysterious.

Ah, but I'm not entirely crazy, just a bit insane. But then again, who isn't? I ponder the term *battling demons*, and while perhaps a bit clichéd, it is accurate. I feel as if every day has become a battle of one state of mind with another, of one reality with another, of one voice with another, of one "neighborhood" of my mind with another. It's as if there are warring gangs having drive-by shootings and knife fights within the walls of my head. There may even be some mental graffiti somewhere in there. And it strikes me that, like our inner cities, this constant fighting, along with the inherent despair and pain that inevitably ensue, is beginning to take its toll and be evidenced externally as a degradation of the city as a whole. This fighting needs to stop. There needs to be peace.

The above is obviously reflective of a man who is struggling with life and with himself. And that man was suffering greatly, not only with tortured thoughts, but with life-crushing, chronic pain— each feeding the other in a cycle of misery that seemingly had no end.

So as I muddled through life, I continued to educate myself about all kinds of things, believing that somehow intellectual knowledge was the key that would set me free.

I once thought intellectual knowledge was the way to peace but have since learned it is the way of the heart that leads us home. It is as impossible to think oneself to happiness as it is to buy oneself happiness. Happiness does not reside exclusively in the brain; it does not represent a given biochemical ratio or quantity. Happiness arises from acceptance, joy, and awareness. True joy arises from an *experiential* knowledge of divine Love.

Intellect, not tempered by heart-centered reason, more often than not is what leads us to hell, not heaven; countless are the paths to both places. Our society has a predilection to believing intellect and technology will somehow cure us from all our ills, that our ever increasing intellectual/technological knowledge will deliver us from all of society's frailties and evil. But our greatest problems are not intellectual problems; they are not societal as such, to be solved by more rules and regulations, whether ordained by government or religion. Our ills, at their root, are always spiritual, only to be recognized and truly solved at the level of the heart.

Intellectual knowledge is so often a distraction from truth. The more cluttered we become with facts and figures which can only describe the illusion we think is our reality, the farther we get from our intuitive hearts. The knowledge of the heart and an understanding of its language reflective of the true nature of and reason for existence is power beyond measure. This is because intellectual knowledge can only describe life as we know it based on our infinitely simple and narrow worldview. It can only describe what is seen and known by the senses, which is but a sliver of the whole. Heart knowledge, defined by intuition and emotional intelligence, is limitless and capable of excursions into the unseen world of spirit, expressed as Love.

In my vain search for truth, studying physics, biology, and other sciences of all sorts, I attempted to learn the answers to the big questions. But I, like many who worship solely at the altar of science, was lost. How did the universe begin? How did life start? What is all this about? I wanted to discover the nature of life, the reason for me and my world, and I trusted and hoped science and academia would have the answers. And of course, I was disappointed. It was the mother of all wild goose chases; there were tidbits coming from here and there, some conflicting, and others painfully superficial, but all were indicative of the ego's predisposition to rampant division, categorization, and compartmentalization. There was no explanation and framework with which to explain with any sense of cohesion what I wanted and needed to know. And while some of the things we are told about the workings of the physical world are interesting in a curious sort of way, the important questions are forever left unanswered. In fact, they're rarely asked.

I realize now they—those who trust only intellect and evidence based outcomes—aren't even aware of the question. Or they find it not worthy of asking due to the fact empiricism is impotent in such realms. Those who study creation by dissecting the minutiae of mechanisms inherent within its complexity will never find truth, at least not within any significant or meaningful context. Intellectual knowledge is a forever moving target; it is dependent on conditions and the perceptual content and acumen of the observer. "Rational science" makes no room for the level of consciousness of the observer, so all that is ostensibly "proven" is merely the product of lowest common denominator perception: what is observable to all within a given material context. But there is so much more to us than our common material experience. Because of this, material knowledge changes. It morphs and moves based on many interdependent factors, biases, opinions, and the whims of society. Truth, however, does not. Truth is truth. It is not dependent upon the acuity of its perception. It simply is, was, and always will be. It isn't complicated, because there is only one truth.

In March 2007, by coming in contact with something beyond normal, everyday perception, I opened my spiritual eyes to the truth always present, just ignored. Internally, I shifted from hard to soft, from rigid to flexible, from intellectual to intuitive, from seeing black and white to reveling in and celebrating all the colors in-between. I now communicate with my world and my life with heart-centered, Love-based, intuitive reason, not with the little voice in my head. And having moved from intellectual perception to that of the heart, I no longer feel the need to ask the questions regarding the mechanistic world ... and I have been set free. There is much freedom in no longer feeling the need to know everything, in accepting life for what it is, as it is, in embracing the mystery, the magic, and wonder without needing to intellectually qualify and categorize everything. What a gift it is to be able to sit quietly amidst the madness and be able to see the beauty and glory of it all.

Plato said, "Science is in no way a search for truth, it is merely the establishment of a means of interpreting our world from one perspective." And I find that one perspective unbelievably limiting, sometimes laughable, and in reality, often meaningless. I no longer look to science to understand life, the universe, or how supernovas work. I don't need to know how life and all its observable phenomena work on a mechanical level; I simply know it does. I no longer look for answers from others as to what my reality is or should be; my heart already knows what is real, important, and relevant to my reason for being, on a level far beyond this one life. The temporal human mind cannot answer questions beyond those which lie within its rather limited perception, and all the big questions and their answers dwell within this realm. The heart and spirit suffer no such limitations.

It is within the grand illusion of fear inspired by reliance upon intellect, without awareness of the higher truths, which creates us and them, black and white, and good and bad. It is the egoic mind that attempts to separate the inseparable, causing pain, violence, and suffering. It is a false dream of utterly self-imposed limitation that keeps us in chains. The reality is that we are much freer than we ever dare to dream.

And where has this illusion led us? To a place of, as Thoreau put it, "quiet desperation," where depression, anxiety, and addiction are common and accepted states of being and where mindless and pointless suffering is the normal state of affairs, distinctly human. A place where dissatisfaction is constant, causing us to vilify our neighbor, while living lives separate from our own hearts and alienated from our own beauty. A place where we believe a pill of any sort will help us actually be healthier or happier—a sterile, dull, jaw-clenching place not conducive to life.

I found my way out of this maze of desperation through some life-altering events that I was not actively or consciously seeking. My ego had a near-death experience and I emerged at peace with myself, my world, my life, and my God. Since then, I have not been able to shake the feeling these things happened for reasons beyond my own personal healing.

After five years of living in this new way, and after receiving sign after sign I was supposed to be sharing this with others, I have finally overcome my own vestiges of egoic self-doubt to tell my story. It all started with something called craniosacral therapy.

# Chapter 3

## The Death of My Companion

The morning started like so many others.

About 4:00 a.m., what should have been the peaceful sanctuary of sleep was once again disturbed by an unwelcome yet familiar invader. The entity would arise from the shadows and violate me in a profoundly intrusive way, beginning with the sensation of a red-hot poker being driven into my lower neck, as if right into the bone. This would set off a cascade of misery, which would escalate unabated and without mercy to heights of suffering I couldn't comprehend. Sometimes, I would lie in the darkness and feel its presence lurking just out of sight ... waiting. Then I'd watch as it approached, growing larger, looming like a freight train, massive and unstoppable. I would sometimes sense this thing was alive, an entity of unknown origin, capable of malice and forethought, existing solely to make me miserable. It would punish me as if I deserved it, and eventually, I began to feel as if I did. It needed attention and was not shy about getting it, and it needed to be fed. And feed it would, voraciously, on my sanity.

After a half hour or so of tossing and turning and fighting in vain to find a position of comfort, I would be forced to relent, the pain having now ascended to the point where I could not continue with any hope of rest. Usually with a moan and a somewhat less than masculine whimper, I'd fight to sit upright as searing pain pulsed through my neck and upper back.

And as I had every night for years, I would sit in the dark, completely alone except for my unwanted companion. Sitting up straight was impossible as my upper back, neck, arms, and shoulders would profoundly ache and throb with any movement. So I'd lean in whatever direction felt tolerable and wedge pillows or blankets wherever I had to, simply to find a modicum of comfort. I would sit in the cold darkness of my living room, staring into the dark void outside the window and into the emptiness which had become my life.

How did I get here?

Like so many people, I was no stranger to pain. For over twenty years, I had dealt with chronic neck problems, and for the most part, I'd been able to compensate enough to function at a reasonable level. But it was always there, affecting the quality of my life in countless ways, some obvious and some subtle but all equally hurtful and disruptive. And as I would later realize, it was wreaking havoc on other parts of me in ways I could scarcely understand.

Whether it was the car accident—a high-speed, head-on collision in 1980—or some unlucky twist of fate combining genetics, a childhood mishap involving a rocking chair, or even birth trauma, it simply didn't matter anymore. Many different practitioners of various disciplines, including all the usual suspects—general practitioners, orthopedic surgeons, physiatrists, physical therapists, and chiropractors—had offered their opinions, and all seemed plausible. In the end, however, it was all pedantic and irrelevant as the treatment plan never varied, and my condition never improved. So I trudged on, feeling alone and helpless, waging war within myself and plunging ever farther into a deep dark hole, one from which escape seemed less and less likely.

Over time, I found myself spending an increasing percentage of my life totally disabled with pain, and at least one week out of every month I would be reduced to lying on my back in such a debilitated state that I could not lift my head off the pillow. The only way I could move it was by grasping my hair with both hands, taking a deep breath, and lifting as if it was dead weight in an effort to simply reposition an inch or two. I spent many hopeless nights crying in agony and frustration while my wife would listen helplessly. She would tell me I would moan and whimper even in my sleep. I felt so isolated and so alone, and I became more and more so as the medical community continued to be without an answer.

Although I was always in pain, I was able to function most of the time. I suffered daily, but I got by—until one day in October 2003, when a new chapter of suffering would begin.

While working as a technician in a hospital, I was pulling a very heavy bed down a hallway when a lightning bolt struck me down. Between my shoulder blades, the most intense pain I've ever felt brought me to my knees and to tears.

An MRI revealed cervical disc extrusions C5-6 and C6-7, and I was referred to a physiatrist/spine specialist and later an orthopedic surgeon. I was placed on narcotic analgesics and muscle relaxers and was not able to work. Surgery was not indicated, but the physicians informed me it would probably be inevitable at some point. Physical therapy was ordered, and I did it faithfully *for months*.

The pain eventually moderated from its zenith, as it usually did, mostly due to the passing of time, but it was apparent it was not going to revert to where it was before. I now hurt all the time, and disabling flares were more common than ever. The numbing haze of opioids became a familiar state of consciousness as I stumbled and struggled daily through what had insidiously become a nearly unbearable nightmare of a life.

In the fall of 2006, I was near the bottom and slowly suffocating. I hadn't been able to sleep through the night or in my own bed for three years. For whatever reason, the couch was the only place I could find which was tolerable, if only for a few hours at a time. Most nights I would go to bed around 10:00 p.m. and sleep for a couple of hours, until I was awakened by *it*—my ever faithful and dreaded companion who, if anything, was punctual. I would get up into a chair and watch TV or read until the pain moderated somewhat, and then I'd attempt to lie down again. After a few more precious hours of sleep, I would be forced up with excruciating pain in my neck, upper back, and shoulders. This was an every-night routine.

Every morning, it took several arduous hours to get moving and have any strength or range of motion in my upper extremities; it felt as if there was a giant hand wrapped tightly around my upper body, attempting to squeeze and extinguish what little life was left. I would sit in my chair wrapped in a blanket and stare at the TV, too numb to even be depressed. When it got to the point I could not lift a carafe of coffee with one arm, I knew I was done. Here I was, a man of decent size and formerly of decent strength and power, in what should have been the prime of life, and I could not lift a carafe of coffee. I was rapidly declining to where I would have to rely on others for the simple activities of daily life, and my wife would have to take up the slack even more than she already had. Into the void, I sank even further.

I bounced from job to job for obvious reasons and gained a significant amount of weight. Intensely depressed, these things together produced a man who was numb and completely lost in the wilderness of his own existence. I did not care if I lived or died. As I wandered around in this personal prison, the image of a gun was never far away. Of course, I never seriously considered ending my life in such a manner because I could never do such a thing to those who loved me, but I did understand the appeal of the idea of escape at any cost. To now face the fact I have tasted such despair to even contemplate such an act is both terrifying and humbling.

My wife was suffering as well, in her own way. She witnessed her husband slowly dying in a sense and was totally helpless. One day she recommended I go see a local MD who did acupuncture because this was one thing I hadn't tried. I resisted because I was tired of doctors, and at this point, I didn't care enough about myself to make the effort. But I was in such pain that I figured at least maybe I could get some chemical help …

I had resisted narcotic medication for a very long time and had suffered through years of pain. But since the incident in 2003, I relented to the numbing palliative approach which equated to surrender in my mind. I now had little hope the etiology of this pain would ever be discovered or understood, let alone successfully treated, and I was weary both of the pain and of life. So if they were going to give it to me, I was going to take it.

After a month or so of acupuncture with no real benefit that I could discern, the doctor suggested we try physical therapy. I resisted. It had never worked before, and it seemed a waste of time and resources, but for some reason, I thankfully and fatefully agreed.

My doctor mentioned a particular therapist who did something called "that cranial sacral thing." She did not explain what this meant; I don't think she really knew. I am a medically trained person well versed in the terminology, so I put it together and assumed the therapist probably specialized in disorders of the spine. I made an appointment with no real expectations. Little did I know that my entire life was about to be changed forever.

In the simplest of terms, craniosacral therapy (CST) is a very powerful, light-touch therapy that releases restrictions in the body's craniosacral system (the membranes and cerebral spinal fluid surrounding the brain and spinal cord) for the purposes of pain relief and overall health enhancement. But as a client and CST practitioner, I can say with authority that it is so much more. CST is capable of profound physical healing, yes. But in my case and many others it does so through nonlinear and indirect means (i.e., by leading one to some form of spiritual healing). By helping a person access deeper states of awareness of his or her body and internal landscape, physical, emotional, and spiritual restrictions and blockages are accessed, learned from, and then ideally released. This often leads to profound insight into the higher truths regarding one's journey through life.

But at the time I got on the table for my first treatment, I knew nothing of CST. I thought this was going to be just another physical therapy experience in which I would be given exercises and stretches and I would faithfully yet dispassionately do them. And then, after several weeks of the same old thing, my current state of misery would be little affected. I had no idea regarding what was about to happen to me. I had no inkling of the power of what was in store or the beauty and the transformational nature of what I was walking into. Ignorance was indeed bliss. The element of surprise was essential.

After the typical interview to gain insight into my history, the therapist had me lie on my back on the table. The room was different from my previous physical therapy experiences in that it didn't resemble a medieval torture chamber. There was no strange exercise equipment, no ropes or pulleys, and no ridiculously huge rubber balls. Just a soft table in a softly lit room.

She began by simply slipping her hands under my lower back. I stared at the ceiling, making small talk, not really engaged or aware of anything in particular, when suddenly I began to cry. I thought this was strange, but even stranger was the therapist didn't seem surprised. No thought or emotion preceded this expression; this was coming from somewhere very deep. It wasn't a sad cry. It was a healing cry, a cleansing cry. I apologized for my display of emotion. I thought it was out of the ordinary, and to me it was, but she simply said, "That's okay. It happens a lot in here." I remember thinking, *What the heck does that mean?* I would soon learn.

Over the next few months, tears became commonplace, as did amazing physical experiences. Parts of my body would move, without *any conscious input*, into positions I couldn't believe. I'd do leg lifts and hold them for much longer than I ever could consciously, sometimes for minutes; I would curl into the fetal position and then uncoil and stretch far beyond anywhere I thought my body could go—muscles strongly flexing, twisting, and then relaxing. I could feel my joints and tissues pulling, stretching, and aligning themselves in a palpable, gentle, and deeply therapeutic way. An unseen force would pull my arms above my head to the point it felt as if they would be torn away. I could feel hands wrapped around my wrists, but there were no hands there. Not physically anyway. My neck would flex, contort, and bend, and my head would turn all the way one direction then the other, way past where common sense says it should—all completely on its own. I watched my body doing this without any input or control from me, and I felt separate yet deeply present. I was simply an amazed witness.

As I observed all this, I began to think, *If I wasn't controlling these movements, who or what was?* It was apparent the motion was intelligent and purposeful; it was smooth and controlled so something had to be in control, yet I was sure I wasn't. Then it dawned on me. Without doubt, there was an intelligence working here which existed *outside* my thinking mind, out of conscious control, yet it was still a part of *me*. It was a wonderful, essential, and, until now, unknown part. This was a life-changing revelation. There was a living force dwelling within that had gone unnoticed for over forty years. It was an intrinsic and infinitely intelligent force far beyond intellect, far beyond science, far beyond human reason, which was closer to me than my own face all these years. And until this moment, I had never been aware of it.

The door had been opened. And by being able to suddenly see the wonder of my own body, a door was opened to seeing so much more.

It hurt at times, but in the best of ways, and as it continued, I became more and more amazed at what was happening inside. Frequently, I would be so mentally scrambled and physically spent after a session I'd be forced to sit in my truck for an hour before driving home. In a profoundly peaceful state, I would stare into the woods adjacent to the clinic, wide awake but numb and pleasantly disconnected—blissful—and I would wait until it felt safe to drive. I had a powerful sense I was being "rebooted."

It was obvious there was a reorganization and reintegration taking place at the deepest levels.

Something strange, beautiful, and somehow timeless was happening, and all areas of my life were being positively affected. My body felt more alive and healthy than ever. Things as routine as walking became more fluid, and I felt lighter in every way; my feet began to fall upon the earth with sureness and a grace I had never previously known. Epiphanies tumbled freely out of the dark, realizations became routine, and everything I thought I knew about my life was not simply wrong but was now completely out of context with the reality being shown to me in the strongest of possible ways. Life began to feel dreamlike and sparkling with a delicate and effortless quality I had never known. My neck pain of twenty years was completely gone, as were all the little aches and pains. In just a few weeks, craniosacral therapy had accomplished more than over twenty years of doctors, therapists, chiropractors, pills, X-rays, MRIs, injections, and everything else—*combined*. And it did so with nothing more than a gentle and well-intentioned touch.

A peeling of the onion had occurred. Layer after layer of physical and emotional garbage was processed and removed in a very specific order not controlled or determined by my thinking mind. And it became very apparent that my emotional scars and the judgments I held were at the heart of nearly all my physical dysfunction.

It seems the layers of "stuff" we accumulate simply through the act of living in such a challenging and often insane world need to be removed in a certain order. One layer must be dealt with and processed in order for the next to be, and so on. One layer's removal sets the stage and readies the environment for the next. And as things progress and more and more of the detritus of the nightmarish illusion are removed, the more genuine awareness becomes available. The broader and more accurate one's awareness becomes, the more one is able to truly see.

I relived and reconciled the trauma of witnessing my good friend die on the side of a road in Mexico, the result of a single car accident. I dealt with and let go of the fear I was holding regarding my own serious car accident when I was a teenager, an incident where I felt unbelievably helpless and scared not only for me, but also for my mother, who was driving at the time. A big part of my process was coming to grips with all the judgments I had regarding my perceived failures, including the anger I felt subconsciously because my life wasn't what I thought it should be or what others thought it should be. I released the deep resentment, regret, and anger I carried for years regarding myriad things in my past—stupid mistakes, all silly and none worthy of the kind of merciless punishment and retribution I inflicted upon myself.

All these things conspired to clog up my system, to keep me from being able to truly see, live, and love. And all these things lived in the tissues of my body. All had physical effects, all were causing some kind of pain, all were making me sick in some way, and all were released physically and profoundly in fits of tears—long, drawn-out sobs coming from places I never even knew existed within me. I could feel my despair pouring out into the room and into the heavens, there was a palpable sense of it being physically released. At times, I could almost sense there was a loving being somewhere in the room, whispering, "It's okay. Give it to me. You don't need this anymore." And give it away I did, over and over again.

Then one day in March 2007, my entire life—everything I had known, done, said, felt, and thought was brought together into a single point of experience and released. During my seventh or eighth treatment, I caught a glimpse of something sacred, something infinitely beyond all my previous experience, something that changed me fundamentally. But first I had to suffer just a little more.

I'd already had complete and total pain relief, which in and of itself was a miracle; I never thought that was possible. I'd also experienced many things which didn't fit my knowledge as a medical professional and rational skeptic of all things not directly seen or proven by science. Life felt dreamlike; all the incredible things happening to me just didn't seem real because they were so far out of my normal understanding of what life was. I remember explaining to my wife that what was happening in that room every week was so far out there, so far beyond anything I'd ever thought possible, it was akin to waking up one morning with a spaceship parked in the front yard, with the proverbial little green man standing there, hand stretched out, and introducing himself. But even that doesn't go far enough. It was a paradigm-shattering, indescribably moving, and an utterly *transcendent* experience. And this was before the day my heart was truly opened.

And this is where I run into trouble—translating what a craniosacral treatment can feel like into mere words. I will attempt to relate it as simply as possible. I don't claim to know the precise mechanisms inherent in the process. I don't think anyone does or can. All I can do is relate my individual experience from my heart. All I can be sure of is my experience.

During therapy, there are times when symbolism is used to communicate between levels of being. And by that, I mean things can happen, and messages given in a very real and physical way that can be symbolic of the issue at hand. What is happening during a CST session is beyond conscious thought; therefore, it is occurring beyond human language, so communication must happen in other more universal ways. Much like dreams, the subconscious and nonconscious[2], communicate wordlessly via emotion, sensation, and symbolism. In my opinion, miracles happen when a connection is made between these deeper levels of awareness and the conscious thinking mind.

Because it works in a nonlinear, nonintellectual fashion, having a completely open mind and heart is imperative to its success. In order for the process to unfold, one must *allow* what is to happen to actually happen. In other words, one has to get out of the way in order to travel to the deeper places where the problem truly originates and where true healing does as well.

That March day, during a particularly intense and vigorous treatment, I was suddenly crushed and held completely immobile

---

[2] A place beyond ordinary consciousness that is not accessible to one's awareness, such as within the tissues of the body, perhaps explaining how and why my body moved without any conscious input from me.

by an invisible force. Unable to move anything other than my eyes, every inch of my body, every single hair, was pressed into the treatment table with such force I feared being squashed like a bug. The force was so powerful and so thorough in its coverage of me it was as if I was being covered with a thick shroud of solid lead.

I resisted and struggled to the point of tears, fearing the immense power of whatever this was. But while my mind was frightened, a deeper part of me was not. Somehow, this part knew there was a very good reason for what was happening. It *knew* this was necessary; it *knew* this would lead somewhere good. This part of me *knew* I had to let go and simply *trust*.

But of course, the rest of me continued to resist as it held me completely powerless and immobile. Thankfully, I did not sense malice in the force; it wasn't trying to hurt me. It almost felt parental, as if it was *doing this for my own good*.

Inside, I pleaded for mercy. It was not a pleasant feeling. I was being literally pinned down by someone or something much bigger and stronger than me, and I just wanted it to end. Feeling suffocated and claustrophobic, I finally decided to stop struggling; it didn't seem to be doing any good anyway. I looked at the ceiling and softly gazed into the space beyond. All I could do was wait it out.

I closed my eyes in a vain effort to escape ... I was spent.

After lying there silently for some time, a sense of peace began to slowly seep into my awareness; all I could do was watch to see what was next.

I didn't have to wait long.

I began to have the feeling of gently spinning in space, but I could feel I was not physical moving. I could sense the solidity of the table beneath me. The motion seemed to be occurring in the center of my head around a fulcrum of sorts, around which all else was revolving. It was a pleasurable sensation, not a feeling of disorientation or sickness one would normally associate with such a motion. It was actually fun. There was a feeling of effortlessness to it as it slowly became more and more forceful and rapid, morphing into a chaotic yet controlled tumbling.

As I held on and watched, enjoying the ride, it peaked and then began to slow. Then, with an indescribable gentleness, it gradually stopped. I rested motionlessly for a moment, floating, when I became aware of motion once more, but this time it was different.

I was now aware of the motion of the earth spinning through space; I could actually feel it moving where the table contacted my back, and I could see its place among the stars. It was sublime. I could sense the mass of the planet; I felt its weight, its unstoppable nature, its momentum. I comprehended its immense size in relation to me while seeing how infinitesimally small it was in relation to everything else. Into this amazing display, I fell ever farther when something even more massive and grand entered my perception.

Entering from all directions at once, this "thing" was all things and nothing; it was everywhere and nowhere. It was the stillness at my center giving rise to the movement that was the physical me, but far beyond this, it was the stillness at the heart of everything giving rise to the physical world. With my heart's eyes, I watched as it shimmered and glistened, radiating light and sparkling in ways far beyond description.

Whereas before I was gently moving and spinning through space, I now had the sensation I'd settled into a groove of sorts, where all movement ceased. I was no longer aware of my breathing or heartbeat. I could not feel the therapist's hands or the table under my body; all had faded into glorious oblivion. I was now floating motionless in a shimmering black emptiness, a gentle stillness beyond description, the most beautiful place I had ever been. I floated within its embrace, timeless, held like a baby by a mother so loving it defies understanding.

Although not actively thinking or analyzing in any classic sense, I was aware the Presence was within and all around me, and I knew it was aware of me. It was given to me without words. I needed to surrender everything to this force, this energy, this entity, this thing of no words. And right then and there, the fight that was my life abruptly ended.

I surrendered.

To Love, I surrendered my struggle and will to fight. To Love, I surrendered the illusion that was the finite and temporal me. To Love, I surrendered my opinions, my knowledge, and any need to be right. To Love, I surrendered my pain, my wounds, my scars, and all my guilt and regret. To Love, I surrendered my will and myself.

To God, I surrendered everything I thought I was.

In a whirlwind, I fell farther and deeper into the black nothingness as my body and spirit melted into one and the world disappeared. Time stopped and became apparent for what it is:

an illusion. My body blended and became apparent for what it is: a glorious extension of spirit. And at once, I grew infinitely large and shriveled to nothing before the immensity. I was completely released and my body grew soft. What I previously knew as "me" had disintegrated.

My therapist knew something very special had transpired and joined me in tears. I lay there motionless for some time, hands peacefully across my chest, smiling, tears flowing freely, letting the sensations of a truly opened heart wash over me like so many waves of warm, life-giving water. I sensed an ancient and sacred stillness at the center of my being. All had coalesced into something beyond perfect.

I wrote this a few days after:

> This was as enlightening and powerful an experience as a human being could have. And this experience, this entire journey, has served to force me to reshape how I perceive my world, my reality, and the nature of myself. My view of what constitutes my very being, my essence, and ultimately the essence of everything living has been redefined and expanded to an extent that I had never imagined possible. I realize now that my body is not just a mass of skin, bone, nerves, blood, and muscle; it is a miracle. Its sum is more than that of its parts. It is alive, and it takes joy in being so. It is beautiful as it is, and it knows what it needs, and it possesses inherent power

and intelligence far beyond that of conscious reason.

I am a lucky man, for I feel I have touched the life force of creation personally, and through this precious gift, I have been pulled back from the abyss and saved. I no longer dwell in the darkness of apathy or the fog of ambivalence. I no longer wander aimlessly with head down through the backstreets of life. I am no longer a prisoner of my body or of my thoughts and perceptions. I now live in a constant state of joy, love, and awe, for I have felt the power of the very essence of life flow within me in a consciously perceptible, concrete, observable, and exquisitely beautiful manner. And now I have embarked upon the ultimate adventure. My life will never be the same …

Wonderful things began to happen from that point on. Food, and even water, tasted better. I heard better, my sense of smell was better, music sounded better, and my ability to create it was profoundly enhanced. I picked up the guitar I had put down seventeen years earlier and played things in a way I never had before; my technique and the resulting music were much more effortless, fluid, and beautiful than I ever remembered it being.

I started seeing the sparkle of life and deep beauty in the eyes of complete strangers. I began to lose the ability to see, feel, and know where I stopped and others began. There were episodes—sometimes fleeting, sometimes encompassing entire days—when time disappeared and whatever I was watching slowed and would move with a very deliberate and indescribably beautiful grace, as if underwater. It became obvious to me that life is like a movie or a play which was being performed just for me, while I was performing for others in the same way. I became a pleasantly detached yet intimately present observer of my life, of all life.

Things were now totally different. My way of relating to people and the world was completely transformed, and the way others related to me had changed as well. People who knew me said I looked different, but they couldn't put their finger on it. Some said I glowed. Some said I simply looked "healthy." Strangers would approach me and ask my advice on life's problems, and without much thought, I would usually have an answer. And sometimes we would sit and talk for some time as they poured their hearts out to me. This was a major shift. I was not an outgoing or extroverted person previously, but now people who needed guidance or help somehow found me, and for whatever reason, I had the words they needed to hear. But the strangest thing was, I had the distinct sense I wasn't the only one coming up with the words.

I now saw all of life, including all the annoying little trivialities, through the lens of a higher and wider awareness, and all was beautiful. An impossibly peaceful timelessness permeated everything I saw and did. With the illusion of time removed from my perception, the pressure which came from always trying to get things done (and never being able to) was gone. All the deadlines, including the one I had erroneously placed at the end of my own life, were now seen as sheer folly. I knew I went on forever, and from this inner knowing came profound peace.

I quickly became accustomed to the rather unusual and entirely new sense of living with an open heart. I could physically feel its radiance, its openness unfurled like a flower to the sun. A sweet and subtle warmth radiated from my chest up through my neck, extending outward toward the heavens. It was a new and welcome companion, forever mine.

Whether I was walking in the woods or participating in life's more mundane chores like grocery shopping, all experience now floated within a brilliant and effervescent pool of warmth and peace. At the supermarket, I would watch everyone moving about in slow motion, walking up and down the aisles, making their choices, and filling their carts. I sensed their spirits; I glimpsed their souls. I watched as everyone, cloaked in all their uniquely beautiful manifestations of flesh, went about the business of living. Each was expressing life uniquely, each was displaying varying degrees of awareness and presence, and each was expressing varying degrees of Love and pain. I watched and became aware of how we are all dancing to a divine symphony—unheard but deeply felt.

I would leave the store and push my cart across the parking lot, feet barely touching the ground. Into the bright sunlight I would walk, feeling the crisp ocean air so deeply, embracing the shimmer of the nearby water, the gulls floating against the broken gray and blue sky. Tears would erupt spontaneously—cleansing and loving tears, tears of gratitude for every moment, for every experience, for every sight, smell, and emotion that has been given me.

Tears, especially for men, are often avoided and even *feared*. They are not welcomed and appreciated not only because of what they may reveal to others, such as perceived weakness, but because of what they may reveal about oneself. But tears are the language of appreciation and forgiveness; they are the body reflecting and expressing the contents of the heart. When they happen due to openness and Love, they are cleansing and indicative of a deeply connected state that can transform worlds.

As the days passed like dreams, I was in such an amazing state of aliveness it bordered on being too much. I felt as if I could fly.

From my journal…

> Just another day of intense growth that's all … This is so profound, and it just keeps coming. I am, somewhat paradoxically, in possession of such endless energy and great peace. Thoughts, ideas, concepts, pictures, and various ponderings fly through my brain and body at the speed of light, all exquisitely beautiful and enthralling. I walk through the forest and I feel so alive, so *connected*. I can perceive the energy and power of life flowing through me. I feel the seemingly

limitless power of my legs propelling me through all the wonder. I can feel the sweet, moist, morning air flow into my lungs, nourishing every cell, and I can feel the rush of blood within me carrying energy and dissipating waste, my heart pumping effortlessly in the rhythmic dance of life. I can feel every cell working perfectly as intended, transmuting stored solar energy into thought, movement, and consciousness. I am struck by an overpowering yet sublimely elegant perception of the intricate and perfect interrelationship of everything. Finally, I shout to the sky … I am truly *alive!*

If the above sounds as if it was written by somebody who is in love, it was. I was in love with life.

Life became not an end in and of itself. I now recognized it as a process of being, a spiritual process that was ongoing. Whether we know it or not, all experience is spiritual in nature; all life is created and sustained with purpose. It is intrinsic, essential, and inseparable from what we are. The choice can be made to live in ignorance of this. One can live unaware of the light and play within the relative darkness of the illusion, as many do, and that in itself serves its own learning purpose. But there is a higher part of ourselves always watching, lovingly aware of the errors and patiently waiting for us to finally come home to who we truly are, to come in out of the cold rain.

It soon became apparent an immense amount of new knowledge, which I have since come to know more accurately as awareness, was somehow given to me through this process. Somehow, I suddenly knew things of which I had no knowledge prior. In quiet times, I found myself asking, "How can this be? What in the heck is happening to me?" I'd lie awake in bed wondering what this was all about. I would doubt whether it was even real. At times, usually late at night, fear and doubt would creep in. I was not supposed to know these things. This was somehow special knowledge. It wasn't for me. I feared I would not be able to live up to the responsibility of being in its possession. I was not special. I was not chosen. I didn't read spiritual books. I wasn't religious. I had no interest in the esoteric or spiritual realms. I didn't ask for this. So why me?

It is obvious to me now this knowledge is present in all hearts. It is inseparable from us. It is the essence of life itself. It is deeply and indelibly imbued within every living thing at the moment of creation. It is always there. It is just that we humans, through countless and sometimes very inventive and imaginative means, have become experts in burying it deeply within the illusion of our separation, resulting in all the dramas we so endlessly suffer.

My ego, which I had let run my life into the rocks, was relieved of duty that March day. In its smallness, it had no choice but to relinquish control to the loving immensity which now permeated every nook and cranny of my being, bringing with it a complete and enduring sense of peace. When the hypercritical inner judge was silenced, the inherent beauty of life was revealed.

What I experienced as a suffocating weight crushing me into the table that day was really the weight of all my struggles, pains, and opinions, all my judgments, regrets, and hatred, and all my resistance to the truth that was so obvious now—an ever present truth which lies beyond appearances. The sense of relief in letting go of control, which is really a vain struggle for the *illusion* of control, was profound. And after doing so, the realization was made that divine intelligence had been in control of everything all along, and it was only in my delusion I could ever think otherwise. The knowledge I thought was new was in fact already there. It is in each of us. It was simply obscured by all the stuff I had piled on top.

By coming into contact with the intelligence at the heart of everything, I let go of the limiting viewpoint I had had of me as human. I transcended my identification with the circumstances of my life. I let go of my identification with my body, my pain, and my human faults. And by so doing, I reclaimed my heart. I reclaimed my *inherent,* God-given peace. I reclaimed my connection to the Source of all things. I reclaimed the compassion innate at the heart of all creation and thereby at the heart of me.

Life now shimmers.

It is within this contrast of what is real and what is not that the secret lies. When the transience and superficialities of common, everyday circumstance is measured against, and contrasted with, the infinite peace and Love dwelling at the heart of what you really are, the importance of all that was erroneously thought to be essential will fade like the stars at dawn. Inner peace at this point is inevitable.

With such awareness, loving openness replaces rigidity in body, mind, and heart. All aspects of existence soften and become slower and more deliberate, more thoughtful. The higher and more subtle mechanisms at play behind, above, and beyond physical experience become apparent, and consequently, life is experienced at a deeper, more meaningful level where joy and effortless peace are not only possible, they are intrinsic. Life becomes beautiful beyond words.

The irony is human experience is made more real by becoming aware of the fact it is not real at all.

Things are now in proper perspective. I still play the great game that is life on earth—it is what I am here to do—but I do so with lightness at the heart of my being; it no longer feels so *serious*. Intimately aware of the sacred nature of life and my profound interrelationship with others, I am simultaneously more alive *and* blissfully detached, and therefore I am insulated from much of the suffering by which I was previously defined. Life can now be truly lived and is seen clearly for what it is: nothing more or less than an ongoing process of learning and loving.

In the end, I refuse to quantify or attempt to name what washed over and into me that day. It has no name, and to try to do so is completely pointless. It does not care what we call it or rationally think about it. It just is, always was, and always will be. It is so far beyond names, rules, and judgment that it makes no distinctions because it lies infinitely beyond the realms where all distinction exists. But it is human nature to try to understand by labeling and by putting things in neat little boxes. Was it God? Was it an angel? Was it simply a higher part of me?

The best answer I can give is it was Love, and by being so, it is inclusive of all the things above.

This force at the heart of it all is, of course, everywhere. It is in you and me. In fact, *it is you and me*. It is accessible to everyone all of the time; it is always present. Put as simply as I can, it is Love beyond description, a blazing, radiant light at the very heart of all things, of all that we call life and beyond. It is affecting your life right now regardless of whether or not you perceive it or believe in it; it lies in the perfection of every heartbeat and every breath.

Because perfect Love is our natural state, all that is necessary to know it, to really experience it, is to remove what obscures it. What obscures this inherent knowledge, which is already present in all hearts no matter how troubled, is our old friend: the ego. Craniosacral therapy has a unique ability to subjugate the ego, to quiet its voice, to calm the tumultuous seas upon which one's experience is floating. My experience, the mechanism of which I was quite unaware at the time, was not unique. I didn't know why I was suddenly so peaceful, so calm, so full of profound awareness and Love. But I was aware that contact with the Presence is what did it along with removing the residue of physical and emotional injury from my tissues. This freed that energy for the higher purpose of actually *living*. I felt as if I was given a precious and sacred gift; it seemed I was imbued with knowledge—reams and reams of knowledge—in an instant. But as I said before, this knowledge wasn't given to me; it was *always* there. Contact with the immense Love of the Presence simply removed everything that obscured it.

What happened to me because of craniosacral therapy is a miracle in every sense of the word. To nobody's amazement more than mine, I'd entered the room an atheist and left an hour later a deeply spiritual man. I was not looking for this—consciously anyway. I was completely blindsided by this experience. And I am so thankful for it, because the best part is I didn't know feeling this good was humanly possible.

But by no means do I think this is the only way home. While a craniosacral treatment is always health promoting, feels good, and is usually a pretty amazing experience, I realize experiences to the degree of mine are rare. And when they do occur, they are not an easy thing to go through. It takes a lot of willingness to face the fact you may be wrong about everything you hold dear. It takes honesty beyond the norm to look inward at your most deeply held beliefs, things you have invested in your entire life, about how you live and what life is all about, and then be able to admit there may be another way; that in fact, you know nothing, and that's perfectly okay. It takes profound openness to go to the heart of your pain, to penetrate where it lives and explore its reasons, to get to the heart of the matter in places so delicate, tender, and deep within who and what you really are. It takes courage to let yourself be vulnerable, to tear down the walls protecting your heart, to confront your deepest fears which are held so very close—fears that for years have been nurtured, justified, and protected. It takes uncommon willingness to open yourself and expose the most precious and guarded places, exploring and verbalizing what is held within them, teasing out their reasons to discover what makes them tick, thereby realizing the illuminating gift of discovering what makes *you* tick.

It takes immense willingness, honestly, and courage to forgive yourself and everyone else and to be able to surrender to the one and only truth.

Everybody's path to enlightenment is different. Sometimes, it takes a near-death experience or a life-threatening illness. Sometimes, it happens after years of spiritual practice and meditation. For some, it does not happen until the moment of death, and sometimes it happens spontaneously for no apparent reason at all. But what needs to be known is the inner peace and comfort which come from living in conscious awareness of your Source is inherently yours; it is dwelling within right now. How you get there is up to you. Your path is as unique as you are.

## Chapter 4

## The Forest

I was completely alone and wandering aimlessly in a cold, dark, and scary forest. A land of perpetual dusk, I could always feel the weight of the impending night. In this world composed entirely of shadow, every lonely step was one of futility along a pointless and endlessly meandering path. As I trudged along without purpose, direction, or understanding, living in fear of what might lie around the next bend or behind the next tree, my mind continually raced from thought to thought and idea to idea in a vain struggle to simply understand.

I didn't know why I even came to this place, but upon arriving, I began sinking even farther into the abyss. My physical and emotional pain was gathering and conspiring to push me down into a very bad place: a place devoid of color and without love, a place not conducive to life.

I'd always sensed there was more to my existence than this. A feeling beyond language was always dancing on the edge of perception, but it remained just out of reach. I knew there was peace somewhere within me, I knew there was purpose, and I knew there was a *reason*. I had to keep the faith that someday I would discover me again and be able to extricate myself from this prison of apathy, pain, and sorrow. I had to believe this, just to keep going on.

And through a series of seemingly random events, it happened. I was led out of the mist and out of the cold and lonely darkness. The fire in my heart was rekindled, and my path was lit to show me out of the forest and into the warm sunshine that gives life—the warm light that *is* life.

This is a precious gift, and it's one I'll always treasure because it is the greatest gift of all: the gift of life and the gift of a second chance. And what's so incredible is this most profoundly beautiful and lifesaving experience was accomplished with nothing more than a human touch. This would seem unbelievable, but not to me, because I have learned about real power through this experience. The power of life, the power of connection, the power of awareness, and the real moving force behind it all—the power of Love.

# Chapter 5

## *Love*

The crux of the message given me that spring day was that all is Love. This may seem anticlimactic at first, but this is the plain and simple truth at the heart of all things. The statement is every bit as simple as it sounds, yet the scope of the concept speaks to the hows and whys of creation itself.

To some, such a statement is trite and clichéd. To some, it is hippie or New Age nonsense. To some, it may sound nice and be comforting to be reminded that Love is the reason for everything. It is something most of us intuitively know, but even this is superficial relative to the greater context. To fully appreciate what this statement means, one must look at what we call love in a much different and bigger way.

Commonly, love is seen as what we feel for our spouses, children, other relatives, and pets. We also misguidedly assign the word to material things. But the Love of which I speak is much more than this—to the point there almost needs to be a separate word for it.

And there is. The word *God* will do quite nicely.

Simply put, Love is the vibrational energy at the heart of all existence, which equates it with what is traditionally known as God.

God itself is not directly knowable, but the essence of it is, and that is Love. It is the currency by which what we call God is known and expressed.

So for all intents and purposes, God and Love are one. The words can be thought of as being synonymous and interchangeable, within both this text and everywhere else.

We are cells in the body of God; we are each raindrops in the ocean that is God … There are many analogies, but they all point to the fact we are each individualized expressions of one infinite Love.

Love is the breath of all life; it is God's breath shared with us. It is the fire of creation.

The more loving we are, the closer to our essence we are, the closer to our essence we are, and the happier and healthier we are. The more loving we are, the more godlike we become. And this is no less than the reason for life.

It's within Love's lack that disease, dysfunction, and suffering exist, and it is only through our self-imposed limitations and egoic confusion that we suffer Love's lack.

Love is the only thing that can heal the world; it is the only thing which can heal us. All wounds are created by the fracture or disruption of wholeness caused by the denial of, or lack of, Love within us.

All is Love. Each of our cells is Love. The sun is Love, the earth is Love, and the air and water are Love. Puppies are surely Love, as are children, of course. Ice cream on a hot day is Love as well, if you let it be. This is because all experience is Love if it is allowed to be.

Love dwells within each atom and tumbles along with the wind. It created us and everything else, it nourishes and sustains us, and it defines us.

Utterly inseparable it is, from what we are.

Love is truth—the only truth—and its denial represents all that is false within this and every life. From its denial is born everything we deem, judge, and experience as bad, but in reality there is only Love and nothing else.

Where Love is missing and we live in the illusion there are things other than, and more important than Love we fracture, suffer, and eventually come apart. Where Love is denied, doubted, or pushed aside, the body is challenged, because Love is life and life is Love.

Love is to God what ego is to fear.

The darkness seen in the world is the darkness seen within; it is the darkness created when light is denied. Where light is denied, Love is denied and therefore life is denied, and in the end, we are denied—peace and our connection to the infinite peace we know as God.

Love's opposite is fear, not hate. But this opposite only exists within our world of illusion based on our limited ability to see.

But the effects of fear are, for all intents and purposes, very real, and its power to create human misery seems limitless.

But this again is illusion, because at our essence, we are inseparable from the Love that created us. But we strongly believe we *are* separable, and it is within the confusion of not knowing what we are that we suffer. Immense pain arises from the illusion that we are alone and separate from God and not worthy of Love, from the belief that we are finite, limited, and on a deadline of sorts.

While Love is the ultimate motivating and creating force in the Universe, it is up to us to allow it and let it flow freely throughout our being. We can choose to disallow its life-affirming force by embracing fear. It is within this choice, this allowing or disallowing of our inherent gift, that the contrast that teaches of Love's true nature can exist. It seems that at our current level of development, we best experience and learn what Love is by experiencing the effects of living in the painful shadows of what it is not. We call this suffering.

Fear and the constellation of its associated emotions, which are nothing but fear disguised, are endemic within this world. How do we live in a loving way in such a fearful world? It is our job to simply embrace the light over the dark wherever it is found. It is our job not to fight for Love but to illuminate the darkness with our inherent Love, thereby lighting the way for others to find peace.

Love does not require devotion or to be worshipped, but it does require awareness of its presence in order to do its work. It requires we be aware of what it is not. It does not judge or play favorites. It is not exclusionary in any way. It does not require belief. It requires only awareness, allowance, and acceptance.

It's true that Love is something we feel. But more importantly, *it is something we are.* It gives support and purposeful intelligence to life; it gives context. It is the framework upon which everything in nature and everything throughout the Universe is built.

The Love we have for our spouses, children, and families is really more something we share. We don't and cannot possess it, and we can't give it or receive it as such. It is light. You cannot grasp light, can you? You can only radiate it for others to bask in its warmth, and by doing so, those whom we love will share in its radiance as surely as we do in theirs.

Like air, Love is everywhere; we need only breathe.

What we frequently think of as Love in our world is really its opposite—fear. When we feel jealousy regarding a loved one, we are not expressing Love; we are expressing insecurity emanating from fear. When we feel the need to control a loved one in any way, we are not expressing Love; we are expressing the need to possess emanating from fear. When we feel the need to judge someone, anyone, we are not expressing Love; we are expressing a desire for separation emanating from fear. When we lie to gain human love, when we martyr ourselves to maintain it, when we feel we must sacrifice in order to have it, we are not expressing Love at all. We are expressing fear. When we feel we need more, and we destroy trust in order to find it, we are not expressing Love because Love is already everything it will ever need to be. Simply by feeling we need more than we already have and already are, we are expressing fear, not Love.

Beyond human relationship, Love dwells in greater scale. When we feel the need to control every minute of our lives, we are acting out of fear, and by so doing, we exclude Love from our experience. Life is a flow, an ongoing process like a powerful river or the moon's rise at night. Can you control these things? How are you going to feel if you try? Yet many do the equivalent by trying to control all the circumstances of their lives in a vain search for security in what is perceived as a dangerous world. Holding onto life with all their might, resisting the aging process, resisting Love's presence, and holding onto cherished opinions with a grip so strong the blood runs out of their fingers and the life runs out of their hands, there are those who choose to live with an iron fist and a chiseled jaw, proud of their strength and will. They are proud of what is perceived to be the prudent power of control, until something happens which brings home the fact that anything can happen at any time and that the illusion of control is just that. Life can, does, and will veer off in ways unexpected.

A cancer diagnosis can do this, as can a devastating earthquake or tornado. A car crash can forge lives in ways unexpected, as can war.

There is profound peace and power in humility.

All we own and physically are, the very eyes through which you are reading this, will very soon become dust. Perhaps our possessions may live on for a while with family or gracing some booth in a lonely antique store, but eventually—and sooner than you think—everything that feels so important right now will disappear forever.

What is left after this life? What do we really possess?

Why do we fight so hard to gather, attain, and protect what in the blink of a geologic eye becomes dust? Why do we fight and even kill for what is in truth meaningless? The lesson is that all that you love can and will be lost, but Love itself cannot.

Our hearts and souls, of which Love is their language, motivation, and essence, are all we truly own in the sense they are all that remain after we leave this planet. Even our bodies are ours only for a moment's time. Can we learn what is important in life by recognizing what it is that endures and what it is that crumbles?

What we know as suffering—all we know as hatred and fear—arises from the egoic or false self. This is the mask you wear, the role you play, the illusion you embrace, the dream which seems so real. The great joke is it all comes from what is *not* real. Your heart watches while the actor goes about his or her role living in relative acceptance or denial of the fact Love is the only truth. The inner peace you feel or do not feel is in direct proportion to level of truth you are allowing in any given moment. In a loveless and fearful world, awareness of Love must sometimes be cultivated and nurtured, but make no mistake: it is ubiquitous. It is just that it can be hard to see through the haze of human insanity emanating from the selfish and egoic hell we have created.

I ask you to let yourself simply feel the Love you are. I ask you to let yourself be swallowed by it. Let it rise within you, as it will, if you just get out of the way. Hold a child or a puppy, and be with those beings without thought or judgment. Let them teach you. Even if the knowledge of this kind of Love seems foreign, be assured if you are breathing, it is there, it is accessible, and it is yours. Close your eyes and let yourself feel it in your chest. There is something there. Can you feel it? Maybe it is like a little glowing ember covered in the ash of a hard life, but that faint orange glow is visible if you look hard enough. Do you see it? Gently blow on it and see how it glows. Protect it; shield it from the cold winds of this crazy world. Concentrate on it. Look at it. Notice how it feels and what it looks like. Notice its color and texture, its warmth. Thank it for being there and let it grow.

This is your connection to God, and it has always been there.

Longer than the sun has been shining,
that connection has been there.

Nothing matters more in this life than that connection.

But what keep us from knowing it?

Love cannot ever be destroyed, but it can be disallowed, and we do that through many mechanisms, all ultimately arising from one insidious force: fear.

## Chapter 6

## *Fear*

Like Love, fear is misunderstood and its common definition must be widened. It is seen as simply what we have for snakes or spiders or heights or the dark. And yes, those are fears and rather good ones if one wants to survive as a resident of planet earth. But those fears are simply evolutionary mechanisms of survival.

The fear of which I speak is much deeper and more profound. It is truly the opposite of Love. It is the *perceived* absence of Love and by so being, it is the fear arising from the perceived absence of or disconnection from God. It is what arises when we doubt and don't truly trust God.

Fearful thoughts of this sort are the domain of the ego; in fact, they *are* the ego. In this life, all fearful thoughts can be traced back to a fear of death, or more accurately the ego's fear of its own death, which along with the body with which it identifies are the only things capable of dying.

Like the words *Love* and *God*, the words *fear* and *ego* are interchangeable. This is because *all fear arises from ego*. They are inseparable. Fear is the language of the ego as Love is the language of God.

Fear of this nature is the primary motivator of modern life. We are submerged in it. It is truly darkness imposed by the mind upon itself and the world. It is like an eclipse of the sun. It blocks light, and it blocks Love.

Fear is what we dwell upon this earth to overcome.

Fear is the only thing keeping you from Love.

Fear is counter to you and disallows your Source, which is why it feels so bad and is so destructive emotionally, physically, spiritually, and societally. It is a profoundly unhealthy state of being. The physiologic states it engenders read like a who's who of mental illness and modern physical afflictions: anxiety, depression, phobias, addiction, and chronic stress-related diseases, such as hypertension, heart disease, and stroke, along with all sorts of gastrointestinal issues like chronic heartburn, ulcers and colitis. And this is only a small sampling of what fear can do and does.

But beyond the physical fear is what lies at the heart of all that we consider bad/negative emotions or states of being: hatred, jealousy, anger, worry, and all the things these things foster, such as violence, racism, and attack of all kinds. Crime, almost without exception arises from fear. Virtually everything we consider negative or bad within our society is ultimately caused by fear. It is a matter of cause and effect.

Fear begets fear.

All these negative states of being are simply fear disguised. They are all interrelated and connected in a web of doubt and suffering. One will inevitably lead to another, and all will lead to physical and emotional pain and dysfunction, which then will lead to the insanity that we see in our world. It is all traceable back to one simple error.

It is profound to consider the depth at which our problems are first created. Everything we see first started with a thought, and that thought was of one of two basic opposing qualities: Love or fear. If thoughts are conceived with Love, if they are generous and compassionate, accepting and whole, the results will be the same: the world and we will get a little brighter and more harmonious. If thoughts are conceived in fear, if they are selfish and judgmental, resistant and fractured, we and our world become a little darker and more chaotic.

The reason for this is simple. Loving thoughts are of what we call God, the creator of the Universe and all things. Fearful thoughts come from ego, something which you yourself created. Which one is stronger? Which one is borne of the wisdom of eternity, and which will live (if it can be called "alive" to begin with) mere years? Which creates and which kills? Which is health and which is sickness? Which is certainty and which is doubt?

This may seem stupidly simple, but what feels better: Love or fear? Which breeds and nourishes life? Which is perfect, which is whole, which is affirming, and which is healing?

Were butterflies, elephants, whales, and redwoods created with fear?

You already know Love is all, and you already know fear is suffering. You know all this already, but your ego keeps you from making it part of your experience. But when the true light of Love is shined within, the ego shrinks and shrivels. This is what is meant by the expression that *you have to love yourself before you can love others*. But we think it is somehow selfish or a hallmark of ego to love oneself, and this couldn't be more backward. It is the hallmark of ego to *not* love oneself. It is not complicated. If you accept you are *of* God, then how can you not be worthy of that kind of Love based simply on the glorious fact of your creation and existence? You don't need to do anything to gain Love; it is already there always. Has God ever made something that was not worthy of Love? How could that ever happen? Can you see the insanity held within this type of thinking?

If I were to tell you that you already have everything in this life you need, that you already are all you would ever need to be, and that you are in fact perfect in essence, what is the first thing that comes to mind? Doubt? Questioning? Do you feel the need to argue this? Does it make you uncomfortable to hear that? Does it make you fearful or even angry? Do you disagree?

Fear is released when it is truly known, and not simply superficially believed, that by virtue of your creation and your existence, you already have everything, and that the "everything" of which I speak is given by God and God alone. What this means is that even if tomorrow everything is taken away—if your home and all your material possessions were blown away—you would be okay. In fact, nothing real would have changed at all. It is the ego's unreasonable and impossible hold upon everything material, *including your body* and the experience that is this life, which causes suffering and pain, because it is an untenable and completely irrational way of being. The truth is all will fall away, and all will someday die, regardless of how strongly you attempt to hold onto it, protect it, or deny it. The ego's attachment to things outside of us leaves it vulnerable to loss. Yet all things will be lost. So we live in a constant state of protection and fear. Your essence—your inner being, your connection to what created and sustains you—is the only thing you will be leaving with when you die; the rest is all window dressing. Don't you think that infinite part of you, the part you are here to enrich and grow, deserves a bit more attention, or at least a passing acknowledgment of its existence?

No power outside of God can ever affect us. To accept this fact is to be released from the struggles and pain that come with being human. To accept this fact while *knowing* and not simply believing, that you—the real you, the original you, the one who lives infinitely beyond this one life, body and world—will live on forever is to come home again. The knowledge you are *always* cared for, *always* loved, and *always* completely safe *is* inner peace.

When the fight against life is discontinued, one can truly rest within. What defines insanity more than fighting the forces of life? There is enormous expenditure involved in fighting the same force which creates galaxies, and it is a fight you will never win; it is not a fight any sane person would want to win. Living this way is unpleasant and fatiguing and will eventually rob your body of what it needs to stay healthy, and alive. Another way of saying this is that peace is found only within and when all is surrendered to God.

Or think of it this way: Love is life, and fear is death.

Fear is everywhere. It is the essence of our society and it does have a reason. It shows us exactly where Love is lacking. Fear is justified, defended, and even celebrated in this world. Those who dare say they are not fearful are seen as unrealistic and given to false bravado. Those who are not fearful are seen as crazy, which of course is in and of itself crazy. Do not confuse fear with prudence.

At your core are silence and stillness, infinite light and Love, and it is around this core you build what you think is you upon entering this life. Along with your body, you are given a mind to use to navigate the world. It is a blank slate, like a new computer, just waiting to be programmed. And from day one, memories, like data on a hard drive, begin to accumulate. It is upon each experience and the memory of it that the next is processed, and through the lens of an ever changing perception you form what you think is your world—and what you think is you.

As we mature, the seeds of ego take root, become inflated, and become more and more prevalent within our thinking—and more and more controlling. Life gradually becomes more cumbersome, complex, rigid, and by no coincidence, painful. Becoming enamored with the minutia and mechanics of everyday life, the ego seeks more and more intellectual knowledge in an effort to justify its position, to reinforce and confirm what it already knows to be true. Attachment to opinions becomes essential, judgments are continually made, and the (attempted) control of the intricacies of life becomes imperative.

A fully fledged ego is born.

Life is now seen, quantified, and measured rather than felt; something to be conquered instead of lived or experienced. The acquisition of things becomes the goal. Money, romance, material goods, and an intellectual education are all fought for and acquired in an endless quest to win. We fight and sacrifice to win a perceived yet completely false and unnecessary sense of safety and security; we work so hard to get to a finish line that doesn't exist.

If you need to see the difference between ego and heart in action, look no farther than your own thoughts.

In what language do you think? If you speak English, you probably think in English, if you are Japanese, you hopefully think in Japanese, and so on. What does this say about the origins of egoic/intellectual thought? It says that thinking is learned, like language, that it is temporary and finite, that it is a tool only existing for the relative blink of an eye you are physically alive. You only think in the classic sense for a very short time in a very specific way. Emotion, on the other hand, is universal. The anguish a Japanese mother feels when her child dies is the same as that of a Portuguese woman, a Canadian woman, or a woman living on a deserted island somewhere. It has nothing to do with learned thought or language. Emotion as the language of the true self exists outside of time.

But unfortunately, we usually identify the very temporary, learned, and false part as the real us. We live according to its needs and moods instead of listening to our intuitive heart, which existed before we were born and will continue long after we die.

Which do you think is truer? Which is a more accurate representation of what you truly are?

The incessant chatterbox between the ears continues to shape a unique version of reality based on sequences of information and associations related to experience; everything is compared, judged, and categorized, based on what we *think* we know based on what we are taught by others trapped within the same illusion. The problem is the information is often false and irrelevant in a higher, more essential sense. The more we learn, and the more we believe and trust the information we've learned, the more we cling to it, and the farther we get from our essence, our true nature, our peace, and ultimately, our sanity. The farther we get from truth.

The world of truth, the higher realms in which the real you dwells, is unknowable to ego and intellect. Ego is concerned with and emanates from the instinct to survive; it is animalistic in nature, primitive. But unlike the survival instinct present in all other life on this planet, in the human animal it has combined with intellect to form a unique mix of consciousness, a particularly dangerous one.

Without ego, violence is impossible. Murder, suicide, and war are all completely impossible without egoic thought because anger, depression, jealousy, judgment, and all forms of attack, whether on others or ourselves, are at their root fearful, and fear is impossible without ego. We sit and wonder how such things can happen—mass shootings, murder-suicides, gang violence, the murder of children—and we shake our heads and ask why. I can tell you that a person who is aware of his or her essential nature, one who is connected to all that is, one who dwells with the true Love of God within his or her heart, is incapable of such acts. And yes, it is that simple.

Ego looks at life as a process of separation and minimization. It sees itself as bigger if it can make other egos smaller. It sees us and them. The heart unites; the ego separates. And only through the illusion of separation can one attack another, can one kill another. Only through the eyes of separation can one pollute the planet or start wars. Only through the eyes of separation can war ever exist.

In an ancient dance, ego sees others as potential adversaries in the struggle for survival; always on guard, it mistakes simple and benign random interaction for attack, and for every attack, there must be a defense. How dare someone not act the way you think they should? How dare they be so rude or stupid? How dare your lover shift his or her attention to someone else? How dare your employer fire you? How dare someone disrespect you? Prisons and graveyards are full of countless egos that have suffered this mistake. Belief in this one lie is at the heart of what we know as hell on earth, suffered both collectively and personally.

Without a center, an internal and eternal place of peace and purpose within, rock solid and unwavering, an unconditional and unqualified place of unrestrained Love that exists outside of our temporal lives, we are at the whim of life's vicissitudes.

We are vulnerable, or at least we think we are, so now we must fearfully defend what we do, what we think, and what we have.

Ego is hard, rigid, unforgiving, and far from gentle. It does not know inherent goodness. It only knows earned goodness. All its worth and all it values are conditional and, in effect, arbitrary. If we are living unaware of ego's presence and motives, we are in effect unconscious and being held hostage; by mistaking its lies for truth, we are living a lie.

Ego is small, fearful, and defends itself like a little yippy dog afraid of its own shadow. It barks, fights, and makes much ado about nothing, and if anything dares come near it, it will bite. Because deep down it knows it is always in danger of being made irrelevant, ego defends its beliefs to the point of insanity. And its attacks can go in one of two ways: inward or outward.

Outwardly focused ego is commonly seen in arrogance, vanity, conceit, anger, and violence; these are the stereotypical egotists who constantly overstate their accomplishments and knowledge in order to gain acceptance and prove themselves better than others.

Inwardly focused ego is much less obvious yet much more damaging. It manifests in violence against oneself; self-deprecation, endless self-criticism and judgment, self-imposed battering, and berating regarding any perceived failures or inadequacies, and so on. This is where depression and a myriad of physical and emotional dysfunctions arise. The problem here is that this kind of toxic self-talk is taught to us as children, usually by unknowingly fearful parents, and it is unconscious and habitual; its power to disrupt and even destroy our lives is profound.

When living constantly worried about the world, constantly worried about where money is coming from, constantly worried that it can all be taken away, life is lived in a chronically stressful state. Fear and stress go hand in hand, even if that fear is totally unfounded and about things that don't exist. The body responds to imagined threats every bit as much as real ones.

Make no mistake: ego kills. From ego arises fear, from fear arises stress, and from stress arises myriad health problems. If there were no ego, there would be no fear, and thus no stress, suffering, pain, or disease.

To sum it up succinctly-

> The trinity of darkness = Ego→Fear→Stress,
> leading to disease, joylessness etc.
> The trinity of light = God→Love→Peace,
> leading to true wellness, joy and bliss.

Chronic fear, as a way of being, is the most destructive force humanity is capable of experiencing. This is the fear which defines entire lives. This is the subtle undercurrent of doubt and shame which informs nearly all of the actions of many in modern life. It's the fear that we don't even recognize as fear. It is the fear that causes us to work too much trying to reach an ideal that doesn't exist, or to prevent something we have imagined to be bad from happening in the future. It is the fear that keeps us doing things we don't want to do to impress our co-workers, friends, or garner the respect of our peers. It is the fear of the pharmaceutical companies' television commercials telling us the terrible things that will happen to us if we don't use their products; it is the overt and shameless fear used by political parties to garner and maintain power. It is this fear which keeps us worried about the stock market or the real estate market or the price of gold, or what is happening a half world away. It is the fear that has us accept more and more governmental control under the guise of security or fairness. It is this fear that causes us to accept nuclear weapons and war.

When life is viewed through the heart, there is truly no fear. But when viewed through the eyes of ego, there is much to fear because the ego thinks there is much to lose: the loss of loved ones, the loss of things that we think are important, the loss of our youth, etc. We fear not succeeding, being poor, and being hungry. We fear we don't measure up to what others think we should be, or what *we* think we should be. We fear losing our way of life. We fear losing our strength and independence, and we fear losing our minds. We fear losing our beauty, our purpose, and our sense of worth; we fear pain; and we fear death.

And we really fear each other.

Many of us spend our entire lives in the grip of fear. Our days are spent with our minds racing from one thing to another to fear. We actually look for things to fear. And when there is nothing imminently near to fear, we will make stuff up to fear because we think being fearful is normal. When we are not fearful, we actually fear we are missing something that we really should fear!

We fear our success as much as our failure, and we fear the unknown as much as we hate the numbing familiarity of the known.

We fear how small we are while fearing how big we may be. We fear those who look differently, those who talk differently, and those who speak differently, and we really fear those who think differently or dare to celebrate God differently.

We fear what we are as much as what we are not. We fear what we know as much as what we don't. We fear the morning and the promise it holds as much as the night and what is conceals.

The truly crazy thing is that deep down, our egos fear there is no God while simultaneously fearing there is.

We are taught fear. It is handed down from generation to generation by very well-meaning people. For this, we do not and cannot assign blame. They are only teaching what they themselves were taught.

We are taught life is supposed to be hard, that you have to fight for anything good, and that to win, others must lose. And from this is borne an undercurrent of aggression within our society, a deep friction, a mistrust of each other, of the system, and of God. We believe that when it really comes down to it, we are on our own. And this we fear.

We are taught we need to control and micromanage life, and we worry and fear that if we don't control every little aspect of existence, life will somehow come apart. We don't trust life or the giver of it, regardless of what we may believe or say externally.

We are taught either directly or through the actions of others that we are unequal, and from this lesson, we learn to fight. We fight to get more from those who have more, and we fight to keep what we have from those who have less.

We fight to maintain our opinions and to prove them right at all costs, because we mistake our opinions for who we are. Our worth is wrapped up in what we do and what side we are on. And through projection, we make the same mistake with others, thus mistaking their opinions for who they are. It now becomes easy to minimize, hate, and see nothing but the opinion, not the human being behind it.

We mistake equality of being with equality of results. We are equally of our Source without exception; what we do with our lives in this world is up to us. How we allow divine Love to permeate our existence is up to us, as is how we deny it. It is a choice. The same is true of material abundance. We need to embrace the equality of our inherent goodness reflected in basic human decency and compassion and spread the Love we are. And we need to do this equally and without qualification to all, regardless of how they think, look, or act. This is true in *every* racial, religious, and socioeconomic direction. This is Love without fear.

We are taught the wolf is always at the door, that all needs to be concealed and protected. And this, in a worldly way, could be seen as not an entirely irrational fear because we are surrounded by others who, through their own unique brand of egoic fear, will take what is yours and even kill you for it. But this creates a perpetual cycle of fear.

Fear begets fear.

We are taught there is only so much to go around in many things, including what we think is love. We are taught we must do whatever we have to do to get ours. But the question needs to be asked: what is truly ours?

What are we fighting so hard to get? Is it money, a good retirement, food on the table, or a new car? But when these things are attained, now what? There is fear in the realization that after we succeed we may run out of things to acquire, and then what do we do?

When we approach our lives with fear—fear of going hungry, fear of not measuring up, fear of looking bad in the eyes of others, fear of not being all we are supposed to be—we exclude Love from our existence. Fear and Love, like darkness and light, cannot coexist. It is impossible.

We call ourselves civilized, but we are every bit the survival-driven animal we have always been, and we seem to becoming more so. The circumstances may have changed, but the energy is identical and in fact much more harmful and virulent because intelligence, technology, and organization add another dimension of destructiveness.

We are very easily led astray by grasping at what we see at the expense of missing the truth held within the hidden realms where all things originate. We do this in our medical system by treating symptoms rather than causes. We do it regarding poverty and social issues of all kinds by throwing money at problems without addressing underlying causes. We do it with gun control, thinking that passing laws regarding inanimate objects will somehow stop people from *wanting* to kill each other. We do it with our government through overregulation, and we do it with our economy.

Money is not the root of all evil; fear is. Our economic situation worldwide is based on fear. This is because the endless need to acquire money and all the things it buys, whether through overwork at the expense of actually living or by acquiring it through less than morally correct means, emanates solely from egoic fear. This is the fear of never having enough, the constant need for more and more, and the attempt to ameliorate the discomfort of fear by indulging in never ending seeking of material and monetary pleasure. The current economic crisis was caused by a relatively few people who already had more than most could ever dream of, *materially speaking*. These people were willing to engage in practices they knew were wrong to acquire even more "stuff." My definition of greed is when the desire for something overtakes the desire to be decent and/or morally correct. It is when gain is sought regardless of the means and regardless of who may suffer due to its acquisition. Selfishness is synonymous with greed, and selfishness is a hallmark of the ego. Again, cause and effect. We think greed is evil and that it is the cause of economic suffering and inequality, but greed is nothing but a *symptom* of fear. Our economic issues are entirely fear based, and so is the suffering induced by the fear that economic strife engenders.

It is not what we do or what we achieve that defines us in this life; it is how much Love we let enter our experience. And we can be very loving and very successful materially. They are not mutually exclusive. Contrary to what some may think, austerity and sacrifice are not godly; abundance and joy are. But we can also be very happy living in a hut with no water or electricity, if our connection is strong. The point is our happiness only comes from within; our outer circumstances are irrelevant, if we are sufficiently connected to our Source. It is always judgment that makes us unhappy and dissatisfied, and that judgment is unnecessary and arbitrary because our higher selves live beyond it. It is always the allowance of Love arising from connection to our Source that allows us to know real peace. The material situation with which we are surrounded is irrelevant to peace; it has no meaning.

It is the relative importance we place upon the acquisition of material things and the energy behind the motivation that makes it life-affirming or destructive; it is the reason we are doing it; it is *how* we do it; it is what we are thinking and how we are feeling while we do it. And just like everything else, we have a choice in how we approach it—either with Love or fear.

The stronger your connection to the truth at the heart of your being—in other words, the stronger the connection to Source or God—the healthier and happier you will be. A reconnection with life on this level is where miracles happen. Reconnection at this level is where true healing occurs. Reconnection at this level is the banishment of fear. Awareness of life at this level is where the garbage is shed that is clogging up your ability to truly experience what is already yours, without fear and without judgment. A connection with life on this level is where the ego has no choice but to quiet, shrink, and shrivel, turning over control to a higher and an infinitely more powerful organizing force. This act of humility is where true grace lives, and it is from here permanent and meaningful change comes. It is this I experienced on the treatment table.

This is a world of contrast. Like darkness is defined by light, we are defined by the path we choose. The good thing is that regardless of the infinite number of ways we can express our lives, there are only two true paths: Love and fear. One is defined by health, joy, and peace and the other by all that is not these things. One is God; one is its opposite. One is sane; one is not. It really isn't that complicated.

As said before, we are the stuff of stars—each molecule of our physical creation is the result of nuclear fusion born in stars that lived and died long before the earth was a dream. Over reams of time and distance, some of this elemental material came together to be ignited by Love and divine intelligence into you. Given this awareness, it is amazing that we worry ourselves to the point of misery, sickness, and even death regarding what others may think about the way we look, what we do, or what we have. We kill each other for things that don't even exist. How insane is that?

## Chapter 7

# The Voice

Do you want to hear a secret? You're crazy. But don't feel bad. We all are.

We are crazy because we listen to and believe the voice echoing in our head. Often going unnoticed because it has been there for so long, we consider this voiced to be the real us.

This voice has been called many things, such as ego, the false self, inner judge, or critic. Whatever it's called, and whatever its reason, its primary effect seems to be to make us miserable.

It is this voice which tells us we are not good enough while simultaneously overestimating our importance. It is this voice that judges everything in our experience, everything we look at, and everyone we meet as good or bad, pretty or ugly, useful or useless. Devastating the consequences are when this discernment and judgment extends to us. It is this voice which causes disease.

This voice is what causes humanity to feel the need to fight and protect whatever it is we have; after all, there is only so much to go around. This is the voice that tells us other races, religions, and nationalities are different, weaker, inferior, or evil. It is this voice that causes us to protect and attack, to believe we are alone, and to mistrust. It is this voice which allows us to justify violence of many kinds and inspires some to kill and some to die for opinions or material things. It is this voice which causes war.

It is this voice that wakes us up at night embroiled in fear and worry, causing our jaws to clench, muscles to tighten, and stomachs to ache. It is this voice which makes us believe we deserve to suffer.

It is this voice which keeps us in a cage, afraid to leave even though the key is hanging around our necks. It is this voice that tells us very clearly what we are not but does not tell us of the glory of what we are. This is the voice that keeps us feeling small.

It is this voice which makes us do things we don't want to do, to try to be what we are not, and to try to be what others think we should be. It is this voice which causes us to be dishonest with ourselves about who we really are and what we really want. This is the voice of chronic discontent.

It is this voice which causes us to try to control everything in our lives. It tells us that we need to be ready to fight and sacrifice something for everything we have and are. It is this voice that tells us we are vulnerable, that we are fragile, and that we are finite, small, and unworthy. It is this voice which causes fear.

It is this voice which batters, berates, and beats us when we do something wrong, screaming at us that we need to try harder, we need to do better, and we need to be more than we already are. It is the voice that denies us our God-given peace. It is this voice that will kill us.

It is this voice that has caused humanity to unknowingly embrace darkness over light, hell over heaven, and lies over truth. It is this voice that causes us to worship things over people, success over peace, possession over Love, and the illusion of control over the freedom of surrender. This is the voice which lies at the heart of the madness.

# Chapter 8

## *Morning*

As the stars fade and close their eyes and the sun rises and warms the land, we stir and rise as well. And as we fall into our morning routine, it is easy to fall into our morning rut and forget what every morning is: a gift, and another chance.

Morning, which follows a time of dark stillness and rest, can be seen as a time of rebirth, a reemergence into the warm light of life. Every morning, we have the opportunity to see life through the fresh innocence of a child's eyes—alive with excitement, anticipation, and a sense of possibility. And in the dark, quiet times in-between all the noise, while we float amongst the stars and gently whisper our deepest secrets into our own ears, we are rebooted to a place less cluttered, a place where all the superfluous information from the day before can be discharged and the slate can be wiped clean. If our rest was as it should be, we will awaken refreshed, with a new perspective and vigor we can use to more fully experience our lives.

Like an artist staring at a canvas of white or a sculptor with hands upon a lump of clay, you are the maker of your day, every day, and indeed you color and shape every moment. There are an infinite number of possibilities in any given moment to *consciously feel* what your life truly is, to confront and honestly and openly assess the detritus you've invariably left in your wake, and to be honest with yourself about who and what you are. The tough part is to then be able to accept it as it is. After all, *it is yours*. Can you do this? Can you love yourself, your life, and even the world as it is, despite all the perceived shortcomings of these things? Can you face and even embrace your pain? Can you transcend the fear which is keeping you from yourself?

You *are* different today. Millions of your cells are new and many have died since yesterday; your body has aged just a little bit. Your knowledge of life—and hopefully of yourself—is a little bit more mature and complete. And, yes, you are closer to physical death. The world is *very* different today, as these changes are occurring simultaneously billions of times every second in all forms of life as it evolves as a whole in its continual and imperfectly perfect process of divine expression, of which you are an essential part. Take comfort in this and know this is what you are here for—to feel, to learn, to love, and to express life simply through the act of living, regardless of how ugly and painful it has been, or still is.

# Chapter 9

## *Distraction*

Living unconsciously is epidemic, and it is not healthy. We spend untold amounts of money and time going to the gym, eating organic food, and taking every supplement under the sun, yet most of us spend very little time on developing loving awareness and expanding the knowledge of ourselves. We spend more time updating our social media than we do getting to know what is in our own hearts, and it is to our detriment, not only emotionally and spiritually but physically.

We all know the feeling when it becomes eerily quiet—the restlessness, doubt, and fear creep in, but instead of letting ourselves simply feel, we attempt to kill it. We have another drink or another hit, we turn the TV on, we make a phone call, or we take a prescription pill designed to separate us from our own experience. Hiding from the big questions because they seem too big and because probing their boundaries can make us uncomfortable is the American way; it's the human way. We live fearful of what we may discover about ourselves if we dig too deep, afraid to lift the lid on memories and feelings we have so carefully concealed. We may not like what's in there.

We don't want to hear of or even think about the truth; either we think we already know all we need to know through the study of, devotion to, and blind faith in religion or science, or we simply sit on the sidelines, trying to avoid ourselves while suffering a seemingly safe but insidious and disquieting lassitude of emotion.

Either way, we don't want to be bothered with having to actually ponder our existence, to actually figure it out for ourselves, to take responsibility for how we feel. That's too scary, too threatening, and too hard. But this lack of self-awareness leaves a hole, because part of us knows we are on the wrong path, part of us knows there is more, and part of us knows there has to be some meaning for all of this. We deeply sense there is a higher reason for all we witness and feel. It dances all around us always, yet we refuse to see, or we simply can't see, due to the wearing of blinders we have been taught we need.

We breathe constant diversion. We treat each day as something to kill, something to be survived instead of lived, and something we want to get over as soon as possible, instead of embracing and consciously savoring every moment for what it is: a precious and divine gift. We are indeed killing time, and it usually suffers an ignoble death at the hands of modernity's relentlessly banal and insipid noise.

Like a critter scurrying into the dark safety of its burrow, we hide in our own personal nooks and crannies. Alcohol, drugs, power, money, and in some cases, religion, are all pseudo-panaceas. They are places to hide, places in which we hope to find answers, places to try to escape the nagging within that something is missing, that there must be something more. But ironically, these things offer temporary relief from our restlessness at best, and with the subtle certainty of a rip current, they ultimately take us farther from shore.

We are far too busy to be bothered with the higher questions, with the higher reasons for life; after all, Facebook is waiting. We fill our quiet time with cell phones, TVs and music players, and an entire society is born that does not know what resides in the quiet spaces of their own minds. No wonder we are increasingly disconnected. We cannot know God, life, or even each other, if we don't first know ourselves.

It seems as if we've lost the capacity to simply walk without being electronically entertained. What happened to the act of walking being enough? I watch as mothers push strollers or people walk dogs with cell phones stuck to their ears or in front of their face, seemingly fascinated by the glowing display. Where are we if we are not here?

We fear the quiet and we go to great lengths to avoid it and hide from it. We call it boredom. We invent machines to fill every moment of our experience with nonsensical information that we trick ourselves into thinking we need. And as we entertain our intellects with what are really just meaningless games, our connection to our spirit suffers. As we walk, relating to the little machine in front of our face, we are not relating to life. We are not in the moment; we are not present. We become oblivious to the passing clouds, the wind on our skin, the butterfly alighting on a nearby branch. We become oblivious and separated from the experience the child in the stroller is having, or the dog we are walking, and we have effectively separated ourselves willingly from our own experience of life. And as those moments pass, never to be repeated, we become more and more hardened, separated, and oblivious to the subtleties of life's gifts. We are effectively unconscious, asleep with our eyes wide open.

The ego is a master of sleight of hand. It will continually develop things to do and attach unwarranted importance to them so you will keep doing them unquestioningly at the cost of having peace. In our culture, it is normal to be so busy we don't have time to breathe, and we do this to ourselves by attaching more value to doing rather than being. Every minute of every day must be filled with what is considered the business of living. Rarely do we question, "Why are we doing this?"

Many of our lives are ridiculously complicated, and in trying to accomplish the impossible, we become overburdened. There is no rest; even our sleep suffers with overthinking to the point many work in their dreams, if they can sleep at all. We get up early and start running from the start. We eat on the go, talk to family and friends on the go, plan our lives on the go … It is amazing someone hasn't invented a way to go to the bathroom on the go. If there happens to be a break in the action, we fill it with one of the million things that always seem to need to be done. In a hectic race against time, we never quite catch up with whatever it is we're chasing, and this stresses us. The act of always running is itself stressful, and the body reacts by releasing stress hormones causing our heart rate and blood pressure to go up and muscles to tighten, among other things. And the crazy thing is this completely unnatural and physically harmful state is considered normal and necessary to be "successful." Maybe the only way out of this conundrum is to redefine what being successful means.

This state of being is counter to our higher selves, and our higher reason and our bodies reflect this. It comes at the cost of knowing ourselves and why we are here. It comes at the cost of inner peace and genuine fulfillment. We are chasing our tails externally at the cost of truly experiencing what life really is internally. There is a reason our bodies react the way they do to mindless activity and preoccupation with doing. There is a reason why this lifestyle leads to anxiety, depression, muscle pain, backache, insomnia, heartburn, and so on. It is not natural. It is not why you are here. Your body is telling you this by developing these conditions, because you did not listen to the more subtle signs your emotions were telling you for some time.

Ego does not want you to experience yourself truly; it does not want you to know the kind of blinding Love that you truly are. It fears, and rightly so, that once you experience that part of you, the only real part, it will be rendered unnecessary, which will lead to its demise. There is nothing the ego fears more.

What we call God is now, what we call truth is now, what we call Love is now, and these things, which are really one thing, are where all originates, including you. All else is false; all else is illusion. It is only your egoic mind which is capable and willing to embrace and attach itself to this illusion. Your higher self, reflected to you via intuition, knows what is true. It can know nothing else.

## Chapter 10

# Ego vs. Love

Ego is fearful; Love is courageous.

Ego is weak; Love is strong.

Ego is small; Love is infinite.

Ego is pain; Love is comfort.

Ego is angry; Love understands.

Ego is jealous; Love is secure.

Ego is alone; Love is shared.

Ego is dark; Love is light.

## Love vs. Anything That Isn't

Ego is temporal; Love is forever.

Ego fights; Love is peace.

Ego separates; Love joins.

Ego is legion; Love is one.

Ego is illness; Love is health.

Ego denies; Love accepts.

Ego frowns; Love smiles.

Ego demands; Love allows.

Ego is asleep; Love awakens.

Ego does; Love is.

Ego punishes; Love forgives.

Ego takes; Love gives.

Ego needs; Love has.

Ego is greedy; Love is generous.

## Ego vs. Love

Ego is blind; Love sees.

Ego doubts; Love knows.

Ego is chaos; Love is order.

Ego is false; Love is true.

Ego is death; Love is life.

Ego is a prison; Love is the key.

## Chapter 11

# Through God's Eyes

When looking through God's eyes, everything is beautiful. Every little thing is a perfect picture, a painting created by the most masterful of artists. A tree is a sublime work of art, a bird is a miracle ... And as it flies away, the Universe speaks through the beat of its wings, saying all that has ever needed to be said.

The gentle sting of a cool breeze on the cheek is testimony, as is the waving of the grass and leaves in response. The kiss of the sun upon the face is perfection, and it belies the larger and grander mechanisms at work.

Walking upon the earth on any given day, life is felt, seen, smelled, tasted, and heard through the senses, the physical feelers of manifest creation. And in that delicate place within where these senses blend into one, life is experienced in a real and tactile way. This is where perception lives.

We are cells of awareness so the Universe may know itself. All is connected in ways sometimes seen but usually not. Every note sung by one's soul combines with another somewhere to form a chord of cosmic music, and together with countless others, these form a divine symphony. This symphony is the music of the Universe, of God; it is the soundtrack of life and Love.

As we travel about this world, our task is to find ways to create, manifest, reaffirm, and express this Love—for ourselves, for one another, and for all of creation and beyond. This is our mission, our task, and our reason.

When we see through God's eyes, we appreciate all we are beyond all we once thought ourselves to be. We see truly and without judgment, and by seeing with the clarity of God, we see completely.

# Chapter 12

## *Appreciation*

After my experiences in early 2007, huge leaps in awareness continued daily. One day as I washed an apple, it came to me how incredible that little green orb was. I thought about the gifts it held, and I saw how strikingly beautiful it was—its shape, its color. I found myself amazed in how it was storing solar energy for me to use—to live, breathe, move, and love. I thought of the energy, vitamins, and minerals soon to be given by the fruit to my cells, substances forged by the apple's machinery of its own life, fusing sun, earth, and water in an intelligent, purposeful, and loving way. My thoughts then turned to everything it took to bring this apple to my hand, including the people who planted the tree, those who watered it, and those who picked the fruit. I realized the miracle of what it took to get that apple to the island where I lived, many miles from where it grew. I thought about all this in totality, and one thing emerged in my heart: a deep sense of gratitude. Breathing *thank you*, I took a bite. And an apple never tasted so good.

These kinds of experiences, emanating from a deep awareness of the miraculous nature of the ordinary, went beyond being common; they became a way of being. It seems obvious that we should be aware of the gifts of creation, but it seems so surprisingly rare.

We all have something for which to be thankful, not just those with material fortune. Those who struggle, suffer, and are ill have much to be thankful for as well. Suffering is indeed fertile soil for growth. Yes, suffering is a gift. I am very appreciative for my suffering, because without it, I wouldn't have had the profound joy of rediscovering my truth.

Regardless of our outward environment and circumstances, our inner experience is our true fortune; the memories gathered and lessons learned are our treasure.

It starts with the simple.

Are you breathing? Be thankful for the air. Are you thinking? Be thankful for your brain. Do you know Love? Be thankful for your heart. Are you thirsty? Be thankful for the water. Are you alive? Be thankful to what created you, and be thankful for that awareness.

Living in appreciation is a matter of awareness. It is a lesson in living in the moment, in appreciating the ways things are, exactly as they are right now. You are where your attention is. Is it focused on the miracles that surround us? Or is it wandering aimlessly, racing from task to task, judgment to judgment, always criticizing? Slow down, quiet the mind, and be. Take the time to simply notice.

From my journal...

> As I lie in bed in the darkness, I can hear the familiar sound of wind-driven rain upon the windows. The frequent gusts announce themselves with a subtle roar from the treetops, and the natural music outside serves to make me aware.
>
> I first become aware of my bed and how comforting it is to be in it, snuggled up under the covers, warm and dry. I think of the bedroom and the entire house and its construction. I ponder the wood from which its framework is constructed. Where was it milled, from what forest was it cut, and from what kind of trees? I visualize the sheetrock, the roof keeping me dry. I think of the hands that built the house and the person who drew the plans many years ago. Are they still alive? It occurs to me how thin such a barrier is between such comfort and survival and the cold wet elements outside.
>
> I think of the neighborhood and all of the souls asleep, warm and safe in their own little cocoons. What are they dreaming about? I see the entire

city, here on this lonely rock in the middle of a dark and angry sea. How many people are sleeping peacefully? How many are drunk? How many are awake and staring at the ceiling, dealing with inner demons and feeling alone? How many are making love? How many are staring at mindless infomercials, worried about an uncertain future and dealing with the overwhelming weight of regret or guilt of mistakes of the past? How many are in bed and wishing they were lying next to someone else? How many wish they were sleeping next to anyone at all? How many wish they were someplace else? How many are wishing they were *anywhere* but here?

I widen my perception and move upward. I see the little town from high above as a point of light in the darkness, a big rocky life raft in the middle of a cold sea. On this raft, we have all we need to survive: shelter, heat, food, and each other. I see how utterly dark the surrounding wilderness is for miles and miles to the horizon and beyond, and this little town becomes a welcoming home, as much a part of me as I am of it.

I see our island as one of thousands in the surrounding area. I see its relationship to the continent and the rest of the country. I pull out far enough to see dawn racing across the earth toward me, and then I sense all of civilization. I wonder about all that is happening this day, one day in the life of the human race.

For how many will today's date forever be captured on their birth certificate? For how many will it be on the piece of paper which will forever acknowledge their death? How many new lives were conceived tonight? How many of those were conceived with love, and how many were not? How many people are being tortured or brutalized right now? How many are hungry? How many have been murdered tonight? How many fell in love, and how many separated for good? How much joy is flowing from humanity right this moment, and how much sorrow?

The energy chain comes into view. From my own body, converting dinner into the energy necessary for me to conceive these thoughts, to the totality of all animal, microbial, insect, and plant life. All of the energy in the form of food is in reality stored solar energy, and I become aware of the food passing through countless bodies, giving nourishment, motion, and emotion to them all. Then there is the water pounding on my roof and peppering my windows. We are all made of this water, and I find it amazing that this most essential of substances simply falls from the sky, given freely like the air. Right this second, how much water is evaporating, forming clouds, and falling as rain or snow? How much is in motion in the form of rivers and streams? How much is being flushed away in toilets? How many people would do anything to have a clean source of it, while outside my window millions of gallons are falling and washing untouched into the nearby sea? How much water is contained in the physical bodies of all of life right now, and how much is free? I wonder how many other bodies the water in my veins has nourished over tens of thousands of years and what creatures it nourished for the millions prior to that.

The life-sustaining basics and comforts of earthly life are some of the most obvious things for which to be thankful, but they are also the most commonly taken for granted. Water, sunlight, gravity, plant life, breathable air ... It goes on and on; these things are not mistakes, and they are not random occurrences. They exist in a perfect and purposeful balance so you in your earthy vessel can thrive in order to learn and develop a more intimate knowledge of the higher truths. The planet and all of its intricate and wondrous life-creating and sustaining mechanisms are a gift, and that gift is for you.

One bright day, I walked along the seashore, and as the sunlight fell upon my skin, it told a story.

Solar energy, produced by a simple nuclear reaction ninety-three million miles away, powers everything around me: the birds floating by and all the life in the ocean. And this power of light not only enlivens my body but my thoughts as well. And these thoughts and feelings, along with the motion being created by my muscles—my heartbeat and breathing—all start out in space.

It takes ten million years for energy that is produced in a nuclear furnace at the core of the sun to make it to its surface in the form of light. It then takes about eight minutes for this light to travel to earth, to fall upon my skin that glorious summer day. The reaction responsible for all that physically lives on this planet is stunningly simple in its physics, which really shouldn't be surprising. Four hydrogen nuclei are squeezed together under immense pressure to produce a helium nucleus, which (conveniently, luckily, purposely, intelligently, miraculously?) has less mass than the totality of the previous particles, and that difference in mass is expressed as energy. That's it.

Energy that was initially formed ten million ago years plus eight minutes, give or take, is giving life to the thought, emotion, movement, and self-awareness that we are experiencing presently. And on the beach that day, I became aware of the fact that *every* thought ever thought; every piece of art or note of music ever conceived and performed; every insect which has ever crawled, scurried, or flittered about; every bush, plant, tree, leaf, and blade of grass which has ever existed; every heartbeat which has ever beaten in every animal which has ever lived; every raindrop which has ever fallen; and every single thought and act of love or hate which has ever occurred has arisen from this energy.

I quietly sat in the sand, feeling the weight of this realization, letting myself become aware of the life coursing within me. I gave thanks for the sunlight and the food it created for me. I thought of the mechanics of cellular respiration, of how in each of my cells food combined with the oxygen I was breathing and chemical bonds were broken and reformed, releasing stored solar energy for me to use. A living, breathing, thinking, and *loving* chemistry, transforming food into usable energy and physical structure by the timeless, perfect, and intelligent orchestrating mechanism of the life force itself. I felt the rhythmic strength of my beating heart and the pulsing blood within my vasculature, blood which, by no coincidence, tastes of the ocean. And traveling within this vital, pulsing, living, liquid matrix are red blood cells, each containing at their core a molecule of iron, just like the core of iron found at the center of the earth. These are not coincidences; this is perfection, and of it, I am a part. I sat on the beach, feeling at once immense like the stars and humbly small like the ants at my feet.

All this is beyond conscious reason, the subtle intricacies of the mechanics beyond comprehension. The ultimate control of these mechanisms, the overseeing force, the master controller, is beyond the realm of scientific exploration and intellect. Evolution and God coexist and are in fact one and the same. Chance and adaptation determine the distinctive attributes of individual life forms but not the underlying processes inherent within their purpose and design.

In all this, I trust. I know it is taken care of, and I know I am taken care of, and so are you. Life takes care of itself and always has and will, or it wouldn't continue to flourish, despite all our best efforts to prolong it or destroy it. Life doesn't care what we do in our silly little dramas; it doesn't care what we think of it; it is so much grander and bolder in its scope and mechanics than we can comprehend. Life, as an expression of what created it, will always be. It will continue long after all we think we know is long forgotten. To let go of an incessant need to know and control is enlightenment. It is liberation, and it shows a deep appreciation and respect for what we call God. It is honoring what created us and all the birds, flowers, and stars.

And this brings us to true appreciation. To be appreciative of all the material things which make physical life possible, to appreciate all the conveniences and things which make modern life comfortable, to be appreciative for our bodies, is actually an egoic exercise, but a necessary one. Appreciation to all that is for all the gifts bestowed upon us physically shows humility which itself is a powerfully transformative force regarding the ego. But true appreciation must extend beyond the physical.

True appreciation ultimately is the acceptance of God's gift, which is peace. It is the humble acceptance of life as it is; it is the humble acceptance of you as you are without conditions, restrictions, or reservations as well as the acceptance of your fellow humans in the same way.

True appreciation comes from aligning yourself with the Love of God.

# Chapter 13

## Love, Learning, and Loss

The nature of our world is one of contrast and interaction, and this is for a reason. As stated before, we learn what Love is by experiencing what it is not, and by the same token, we not only learn this directly through our own experience but by the experience of others. There is a reason we are all different, so that we might experience and create in infinitely different ways. We express the one lesson—Love—an infinite number of ways.

Life is an ongoing and endless teaching-learning interaction; every single time two or more people interact, there is an exchange of information and there is an opportunity to learn or teach. And by now, we can probably guess what the subject always is …

We even teach strangers in the most casual of interactions, such as the clerk at the local store and the plumber under your sink. We teach what we know, but more importantly, we teach what we are. Do we teach peace, tolerance, and patience, or are we teaching anger, impatience, and fear? What is it you want to teach?

No matter how it is disguised, all experience is about learning; even the most tragic and nonsensical events provide an opportunity. The Holocaust certainly doesn't seem to have anything to do with Love but it certainly showed us what could happen when its opposite, fear, combined with a barbaric willingness to murder and destroy ruled a great part of the world.

I am not speaking of getting up on a soapbox and preaching what you think you know. I am speaking of teaching Love by simply being it. When the checker at the local market is gruff and short with you and doesn't give you the greeting you think you might deserve, try extending compassion to her wordlessly. You have no idea what her personal life is like. She may be dealing with taking care of a sick parent or child; maybe her husband is in the military overseas and she is fraught with worry, or maybe she is dealing with health issues. Maybe she was abused as a child and is dealing with the emotional weight of that reality. Sometimes, we mistake rude or disinterested behavior for attack when really it is a reflection of inner strife and confusion, things we all have experienced.

The next time an elderly person pulls out in front of you and drives too slowly in your opinion, instead of getting angry or impatient, put yourself in their place. Try to remember they can't see or hear like they once did and they certainly can't move as fast. Keep in mind that maybe that person just left the hospital where their spouse of fifty years is dying or maybe just passed away. You don't know what is on another's mind. All it takes is to make a choice to respond with compassion and patience instead of anger, rudeness, and frustration. Every single time this choice is made, the world is a little better place and you not only feel a little better, you *are* a little better.

The reality is we are all trying—we are all doing the best we can. This may not appear so because different people are at different places vibrationally; therefore, they see things differently and do things in a different way. But that does not make them any less than you. To extend compassion to your brothers and to try to love them as yourself at all times is what brings us closer to God.

One thing I learned when I worked as a craniosacral therapist is that we all have things not far from the surface that we are living with and hiding from others and often ourselves. So many times clients would enter the clinic talkative and full of life, proud of how busy they were and describing all the things they had to do that day. They would get on the table, still talking a mile a minute, and I would put my hands on them. And invariably things would change.

It wouldn't take long before their voice would trail off almost as if they were falling asleep, the chatter of the ego would diminish, and then the real person would emerge. And more often than not, something would be uncovered they have been living with for years. Childhood sexual abuse, the loss of someone that was never adequately dealt with, guilt over something they did or didn't do, the fact their lives are not what they thought they would be, or feelings of being frustrated or trapped. It doesn't matter what it is. What matters is that we all have "stuff" we are carrying beneath the waterline. We are all carrying pain, guilt, and regret, some of us immense amounts; we are all dealing with the struggle that is human life. We all feel powerless, frustrated, and afraid at times. It is universal, it is the human condition, and once we recognize we are all wounded, we all have failings; when we honor the fact we all struggle and suffer; compassion can be extended equally and copiously toward all.

We are all equal in our Creator's eyes, and simply by that fact, we should be in each other's. We are all worthy of Love; we are all children worthy of patience from each other and ourselves as we learn life's lessons.

Often the pain caused by any given situation is caused by the judgments we make about it rather than the situation itself. I had a friend with cancer who was receiving chemotherapy and one day she called in tears because she was too weak to empty her dishwasher. As we spoke, I helped her see that she was in tears because of her expectations; she was working herself into an absolute frazzle because she thought she *should* be able to do this simple task. When she *accepted* that emptying the dishwasher wasn't really that important—that it really didn't matter at all—the stress went away, and she felt immensely better. By simply refocusing the little energy she had away from the stress caused by an irrelevant judgment, she was able to use this energy to feel better.

This is ego in action, the act of focusing on something that doesn't matter *at all* and attaching immense importance to it (which is a form of distraction) causes untold suffering. This goes back to the ego's value of doing over being, and the lesson goes far beyond simply emptying a dishwasher. This kind of self-imposed erroneous judgment and the resulting fear created by it was how she lived most of her life. It was what she was taught as a child, and the chronic stress it created probably played no small part in the development of her disease. It took a life-threatening disease to gain this knowledge, the recognition of what is real and important, and how to keep in perspective all that is not. And that's okay. This could be said to be the purpose of life-threatening disease to begin with. She learned a lesson in letting go, in choosing battles wisely if they need to be chosen at all.

The lesson: let go of how you think your life should be and embrace the life you have, regardless of your external circumstances.

Wouldn't it be nice if we could learn such things before we are faced with death?

Cancer is something which affects everyone one way or another, and even the word generates considerable fear. Its progression is usually, though not always, slow, giving all concerned plenty of time to ponder the larger meanings inherent within its process. If all disease is a teacher, then cancer is the graduate program in the curriculum of life and the lessons possible with it are limitless.

Cancer can teach us what is really important by threatening and often succeeding in taking away all we thought was important but really isn't, and this includes our body. From my experience, there are two reactions to a cancer diagnosis, and not surprisingly, it mirrors the rest of life. Its seemingly sudden appearance in our experience can be met with either Love or fear. Of course, fear is involved with any such diagnosis initially, but how one handles the rest of the course follows one of those general lines. There is no wrong or right way to respond; both offer the opportunity to learn.

There are those who get fearful and angry and stay that way; they withdraw and feel as if they are a victim. Then there are those who transition into a lighter way of being, and in a strange way, they actually feel freer after being diagnosed. These are the people who are always smiling and talking to the other patients at the chemo center, the ones who are more beautiful than ever with no hair, the ones whose eyes sparkle. These are the people that inspire others even if they succumb to the disease. These are the ones who in a sense have been set free from all the artificial and unnecessary encumbrances we burden ourselves with every day. They have accepted their place, their state of being, and have realized a special brand of inner peace.

We are released from much of the control illness possesses over us when we overcome this notion that disease, suffering, and pain are automatically bad things instead of simply part of our life experience. In fact, it could be said the preponderance of suffering associated with life-threatening disease is caused by the judgment and fear it inevitably creates, not the disease process itself. It is only our judgment that colors these things with such an air of fear, sadness, and despair, and that judgment is entirely created by us. Therefore, it can be altered or eliminated by us. Life is about experiences that *have to happen*, and in fact, experiences *we create*, in order for us to learn. And yes, this sometimes means illness and death are necessary for growth. If we are still suffering, we simply haven't learned the lesson. So what is the lesson?

Most obviously, any life-threatening situation reminds everyone involved that *this* life is finite, precious, and not to be taken for granted. It is so easy to get caught up in the business and *busyness* of life and forget what a miracle every day, every breath, and every heartbeat is. Love and appreciation are known when conscious attention is paid to the gift of life in all its expressions. By so doing, we honor the giver of that life and bring ourselves into alignment with God.

Suffering, or hopefully the transcension of suffering brought about by *acceptance*, brings home experientially the fact at the heart of it all—we are not this name and we are not this body. We are not what we do, nor are we defined by what we have, where we live, or what religion we choose to believe. We are not our thoughts, and we are not our emotions. We are what lies beyond all these things. We are what exists beyond the chatter of our minds; we are indeed what witnesses our life. We are eternal light, everlasting life, and infinite Love, and we are as inseparable from our Source as much as the light falling upon one's face on a brilliant summer day is separable from the sun.

When we ignore the more subtle cues that there is a lesson at hand, a more direct path to knowing is solicited. If we ignore things like chronic depression, sadness, anger, worry, grief, and fear and we don't take the time to discover and face their causes, physical illness will inevitably result in an effort to shine a light on what needs to be learned.

What a wonderful lesson for those who are ill and all those around them who choose to see it, that it is the heart that matters, that Love in all its forms is the only truth. The fact peace ensues when one lets go of attachment to all things, including this body and this life is the greatest of gifts, and it is one we seem to resist learning with every breath.

Life is always perfect, even when it isn't.

It is a powerful lesson to be able to let go of expectation to the point that even death loses its power. Life is always perfect, even when it isn't, is a very liberating way of looking at things, because it reinforces the absolute truth that *you are not vulnerable to anything*. Of course, your ego vehemently disagrees with this and will always try to keep you fearful and unhappy, but the truth is that all is always as it should be—*always*.

*Life is perfect, even when it sucks.*

A letter to friends and family I wrote during a challenging time touches on this philosophy ...

> Well, this has been the most challenging two weeks of my life, and in all honesty, I am worn out. My mom is still in the hospital and now not doing so well ... again. As it stands now, she won't be going home; she will have to go to a nursing facility for the duration of her life. In the

middle of all of that, my wife's mom had to be hospitalized with complications of her cancer/chemotherapy, and then my dog "Moose" had a drug reaction and also had to be hospitalized. So at one point, we had three loved ones in the hospital thousands of miles apart, and two of the three were in a perilous state. And then, in no small part due to the stress I'm sure, my wife got sick and of course so did I. Throw in all the financial concerns which inevitably arise with things like this, and it is easy to feel a bit overwhelmed.

I know well the universal philosophies *all things under the sun have a reason* and *life will never give you more than you can handle*, but I've never felt so challenged, so strung out, so uncomfortably stretched in all my life. I thought, *What would I say to someone coming to me expressing these same feelings?*

I would say there are always lessons to be learned, sometimes they are hard to see, and sometimes they hurt. Life is always perfect, even (maybe even *especially*) in its imperfections, and all of life is beautiful even when things aren't the way you wish them to be or the way you think they should be. The experience of life is always as it should be, even when frustration, sadness, or helplessness seem to rule one's heart.

That is what I would preach, and I believe it all to be true, but this is what I did ...

I questioned. Why does an eighty-two-year-old woman have to suffer so when all she has ever done is give of herself? Why does an innocent animal have to suffer when all he has done is love everyone and everything deeply and unconditionally every single moment of his short life? Why must our loved ones suffer and therefore us as well? Why do such painful challenges inevitably arise in all of our lives? I posed these questions to the moon and stars, and it occurred to me in a quiet moment that maybe they suffer so we might learn. We might learn to appreciate our own health and become more aware of our ability to feel deeply and love fearlessly, without boundaries or conditions. We might learn to take not one second with those we love for granted and might be reminded their presence in our lives is indeed a precious gift. We might learn we are all teachers and students in an eternal and sacred relationship and that, just maybe, they are not suffering at all, they are simply teaching us what it is like to feel helpless, to feel sad and overwhelmed, and what it is like to lose something we love very much. We need to feel these things as much as we do happiness and joy in order to be truly alive and in order to grow. And then the quiet realization settles somewhere deep within: someday, we will be teacher in a very similar lesson.

Beginning with my mother-in-law's diagnosis of metastatic cancer a few months ago, I've learned many things, as have all concerned even if they aren't aware of it. Personally, I've learned loss is a wonderful teacher. Cancer in particular is effective in that it powerfully teaches this lesson to the one who is being "lost" (in reality they are being *found*) because it brings home what is real and what lies at the heart of it all. How is the value of something measured if it cannot be lost? And if that lesson can be truly learned, peace will forever dwell within one's heart.

When life is challenging and when nothing seems to be going your way, when you are frustrated and angry and ready to burst, take it that the Universe is telling you, "There is a lesson here!" Instead of letting circumstances run you over, slow down and take a look at what may be hiding in plain sight. If the lesson is always Love, look for Love in any situation. I assure you it is there.

Always remember: assume only Love, teach only Love, be only Love. If you do nothing but remember this, you can never go wrong.

I wrote the following for my wife when she was dealing with some personal issues that had her frustrated and angry. She was doing as most of us do—focusing on the problem and suffering the consequences of wishing things were different when the reality was she had no power to change them.

> We are being taught a lesson in present moment living. We are being taught that we need to be aware that life is happening right now and *only* right now. By devoting so much time to looking forward to an unknowable future, we fail to notice our own life is happening right now, and by continually failing to live in the present, we will eventually discover we have not really lived at all.
>
> Whenever we feel frustrated, angry, impatient, or depressed, we know we are not in the present moment because these feelings are created by these feelings are the result of the discontinuity and struggle between ego and spirit. In other words, when we are not living in the present moment, we are not in alignment with our true nature and purpose, we are not in alignment with our essence, we are not in alignment with

universal law, and we are not in alignment with our Creator. We are doing a disservice to ourselves, each other, our community, and ultimately, to all that is.

This is the lesson.

If we stop ourselves from this thinking and consciously descend into the only reality, which is right now, we immediately transition to a peaceful way of being. We realize that all we need for true happiness is always available, right here right now. This is the great cosmic joke. We live most of our lives feeling unfulfilled and trapped in a prison of our own making while the key to unlock the door is closer to us than our own face … and it always has been.

The only way out of the emotional pain, which will inevitably lead to physical dysfunction, is through the recognition of such things. True joyfulness, our natural state, is attainable through one simple act: surrender. Honor yourself, and honor God. Say quietly, "I surrender to all that is." It is that simple, if you mean it.

Realize you are responsible for how you feel at all times. Situations or people cannot make you feel bad, only your reaction to them can. Realize your existence is a precious gift and you can do its giver justice by living in the now, by being grateful for everything you have, and by loving yourself. Take time to ponder your own nature and purpose; feel the infinite nature of your heart and the Love it radiates.

Realize that heaven is everywhere. It is in your own heart and the heart of another. It is in the eyes of a loved one and in the laughter of a child. It's in the gift of tonight's dinner and in the air you are breathing right this moment. It is in the breeze, the trees, the stars, and sky. Heaven is as close as the ground under your feet.

By writing this, she not only learned to look at things in a different and more liberating way, but I reminded myself of the truth as well. By looking for and finding the lesson of Love within the situation, we together transitioned the issue into something positive and all suffering regarding it ceased. Can it be that simple? Yes, it can.

Some of the best teachers are not even human. As I neared the end of writing this book, my canine companion of nine years, my best friend, passed away.

His name was Moose and he was a large chocolate Labrador I brought home as a puppy one day in 2003, a birthday present for my wife. He spent most of the last year on the floor right behind me as I wrote this book; I can still hear him breathing back there.

Moose taught me many things. When he was young and I was lost in pain and sadness, he tolerated my impatience with him, which was really my impatience and frustration with my own life. He tolerated my yelling at him when I was frustrated, and he always forgave me.

Moose was a mirror. Through his eyes, I saw myself, and in the early years of his life, what was reflected back to me was not something of which I was very proud. But he loved me anyway. I realized even then that he was giving me the wonderful gift of showing me just where I needed work, where I needed to grow. He tested my patience at times, thereby showing me I needed to work on patience. By always forgiving me, he taught me forgiveness. And by always loving me regardless of how I looked or acted or smelled, he taught me about unconditional love, and he did so effortlessly.

Moose, by never needing more than affection, attention, a scratch on the head, and some time to play, taught me how profoundly simple joy is supposed to be. He taught me how simple and natural joy *is*.

Moose, in fact all dogs, aren't simply teachers; they are masters of what we need to learn. Always present, always loving, always accepting, and always giving and full of grace, he was an example of complete innocence and purity. These are things to which I, and I would hope most of us, aspire. To him, these things came naturally and effortlessly. They weren't things he did; they were things he was.

Different dogs have different ways of teaching the one lesson. Some sacrifice themselves by being abused and showing us how ugly we can be when our hearts are devoid of compassion, and then these same spirits can show us the way home by becoming healed through the gift of Love's patience, thus healing us. Always in the moment, some become symbols of inspiration by handling disease and disability with unimaginable courage and grace. Dogs by virtue of their relatively short life span will inevitably get sick and die before us to teach us of loss and the lessons learned by encountering it and transmuting it into Love via acceptance. With dogs, we are witness to the entire lifespan of the animal. We see and remember the exuberance of the puppy, the regal nature of the adult in its physical prime, and the physical decline as he or she ages. This mirrors our own experience, reminding us of the transient nature of our own lives. Animals also teach us about nonattachment by dying with grace and dignity.

The day before Moose left us, I got down on the floor face-to-face with him, and we had a conversation. He had stopped eating and was very low on energy, and I knew that tomorrow was going to be the hardest day of my life; in fact, the appointment had already been made.

I stared into his impossibly deep eyes and told him how much I loved him and how much I was going to miss him. I thanked him for being my ever present companion for nine years, for being with me through the good times and the bad. I thanked him for tolerating my insanity and for always being by my side. I thanked him for his unquestioning and loving presence. I kissed his nose, I stroked his head, and he softly stared at me, accepting all I was saying, accepting what was going to happen in less than twenty-four hours much better than I was. I was hurting and it struck me the loneliest walk a man will ever take is from the veterinarian's office with nothing but a collar.

He knew it was time to go; I could see it in his eyes. And when we took him to the vet the next day, he collapsed on the way to the car as if to show us there was absolutely no doubt it was time. I know he was appreciative. He was so calm and at peace; he knew exactly what was happening; he needed to be set free, he had done his work here and it was time for us to stop interfering with his wishes. And it was time for me to relearn and become intimately acquainted with the lesson in the inherent pain of letting go. I can only hope I meet my death with such grace.

## Scars

What is blue without gray? What is night without day? What is life without death? And what is love without pain?

All human life is based upon the contrast of joy and suffering, and all human life knows pain. Physical, emotional, and spiritual injury is an unavoidable consequence of existence, and the scars left behind color and define who we are. It is how we cope and deal with such pain which determines how we live. Do we suffer in silence and avoid ourselves, our own hearts, to the detriment of our souls? Do we relive and suffer within while the stars peer down and watch silently? Do we take sanctuary in the numbing effects of the bottle or pill? Or do we recognize that to suffer is to feel and to feel is to be alive.

I have had warm blood on my hands, and I have killed. I have seen bodies torn to shreds by bullet and car, and I have held lifeless babies in my arms. Who or what would I be without this? Would I be the same person? Would I have the same appreciation and reverence for life I now know?

We are here to learn through feeling and for no other reason. To love fully and without fear is who we are. To suffer is to love, and to hate is to die. We wander with open eyes and open hearts, seeing, feeling, being, and looking for answers for which there are no questions. Carrying a timeless load of what we were, are, and will be, and carrying within all we have seen, all we have touched, all we have loved, and all we have hated. These are the things that make up a life.

We are little bundles of energy wrapped in flesh. Translating cosmic light into motion, into memory, is what we do. We are like so many icebergs: what is seen is so little of what there is. Energy in motion, fade and move around, exploring ourselves and each other.

So the next time the smell of coffee awakens you, the next time you catch a familiar and knowing glint of life in a stranger's eyes, the next time a dog licks your face, give thanks. The next time you fall in love, and the next time your heart breaks, give thanks. The next time you are caught out in the rain, and the next time your heart feels pain—give thanks—because you're alive.

CHAPTER 14

# The Endless Summer of the Heart

Do you remember a time when you were truly at peace? A time when the warmth of life flowed effortlessly through you, when the world sparkled in an endless summer sun? A place where the green was impossibly alive and the blue equated forever?

Do you remember when life was always fresh and forever held the promise of something new? When watching a soaring hawk captivated your imagination and you too could glide upon its wings to see what it could see? A magical place where the clouds floated by, forming shapes just for you while stirring something deep inside—timeless and strangely familiar?

Do you remember a forgotten place where the water's sparkle held the secret of mysteries hidden below and the warmth of the sun on your face suspended time? Where dirt, mud, and bugs were essential connections to life, and the stars and moon were like old companions serving as a perfect backdrop for exploring life's mystery?

Do you remember when time mattered not, when each day was a lifetime unto itself and was always explored with endless enthusiasm, energy, and vigor? A time when there were no deadlines, no need to rush, no need to get anything done? A time when yesterday was ancient history and tomorrow a distant dream, and neither mattered much to you? A time when you trusted completely, laughed more than you spoke, ran more than you walked, and felt more than you thought?

Do you remember a time when you were always safe, deeply happy, and in need of nothing? Where there was no awareness of vulnerability, nothing to protect, no need for defense?

Do you remember how you felt before you learned judgment, fear, struggle, and pain? Before opinions and attachments suffocated your heart, strangled your mind, and removed any hope of peace?

What did it feel like before the separation, when you learned endless thinking and the acquisition of useless facts, material goods, and opinions was the way to happiness? Has that bubble burst, or are you still mad? When did you first learn to categorize, analyze, pick apart, judge, and try to control every aspect of your life and environment? When did you first learn to protect and hide and lie to yourself about the discomfort you feel when alone with your thoughts? How much effort are you putting into trying to control the uncontrollable, to fighting the phantoms in your head, in endlessly planning for that which cannot be planned? How long are you going to fight against the way things are, vainly struggling for some sort of an illusion of safety, some sense of completeness?

Where did it go? I know you know the place of which I speak, and I know you long for it. Where is that place of innocence and timelessness, warmth and complete peace? Is it still in you? If you are quiet, can you feel it in your body, in your memory? Or does it lie beyond these things?

You catch glimpses once and a while—in a random piece of music which momentarily ceases the inner conversation as you feel a sweet tingling warmth swelling from your gut into your chest. Perhaps you have felt it when gazing at an old painting that seems to obviate time as you stare transfixed, gently probing the boundaries of some long-lost feelings. Maybe your timelessness was hinted at when you found yourself completely lost in the blood-orange glow of a sunset or the roar of a waterfall, or maybe in that ethereal state just before sleep when you blissfully straddle two different worlds. But those precious moments are ever fleeting, and the more you try to grasp them and make them last, the more they elude you. How can you reconnect with what you really are?

That child is still within you, with all its innocence and beauty, and that effortless peace. It is still in you and always has been. It is the stuff of which you, at your essence, is made; it is a glimpse of the place from which you came and the place to where you will return.

Isn't it time to stop the insanity, to wake from the nightmare, and to realize it is all completely of your own making? Isn't it time to stop wandering in circles in the dark forest and step out into the warm light? Isn't it time to be reacquainted with yourself, your purpose, your essence? Isn't it time to discharge all that is false, all that is keeping you from seeing, and all that is keeping you separate, alone, and longing?

Isn't it time to recognize and celebrate your gifts—the gift you are to yourself, this world, all your friends and family, to all who will ever know you—to all that is? Isn't it time to realize you are a miracle, you are perfect, and you are all you need to be right now and you always have been? What is it going to take for you to realize to glory of every single breath you take? A hidden part of you knows this truth—that like Love, God is not outside of or separate from you. God is in every heartbeat, in every tear and raindrop, and in every blade of grass. There is no judgment; there is no fear, except that which you yourself create, and it just isn't real.

It is time to relearn how to bow to your own radiance and the radiance of all life, and to the intelligence responsible for it all. It is time to reclaim what is already yours by the virtue of the simple and grand fact of your existence. Part of you does remember—the part that cries when faced with true beauty, the part that smiles without thought upon watching a child play. Relax your mind and move beyond your fear and come back home to your true nature. It requires no effort, just awareness.

Shine the light upon your own darkness. Let go of your cherished solemnity, examine and realize its pointless nature, and then watch it recede and vanish like the crashing water's foam. What was it doing for you anyway, except to keep you mired in the pain of the illusion?

The heaviness in your heart, the chains that bind, can be replaced with the lightness of Love, laughter, and peace, if you so choose. The way is always as close as your next breath.

# Chapter 15

## Expectations and Suffering

Why is it we so often struggle and fight with life, making such immense sacrifices to feed the beast? In a glaring act of self-incarceration, we willingly encase ourselves with cages we buy and tether ourselves with things we cannot afford and don't need, adorning our lives with useless trinkets. Always searching for something we can't put a finger on, we think we will know it when we see it, and once we acquire whatever it is, we will finally be happy.

But questions dance in the shadowy periphery of our awareness. Sometimes, we feel their presence before we push them away. Is life supposed to be this hard? Is it supposed to hurt this much? Is there more than this?

Where is the joy? Where is the beauty? Where is the peace?

To recap, this is a world of contrasts and we learn by exploring the infinite number of possibilities given us in every living moment. On one end of the experiential scale is Love—pure, unconditional, blinding, divine Love. The rest of the scale reflects varying degrees of anything that isn't. All beings, before they are clouded by societal indoctrination, materialism, and ego, strive for this Love. It is what we are, and it is what we are here to know. Some call it God, some Source. It is known by many names, but whatever you want to label it, it is what created you and butterflies and supernovas. It is all there is; all else is false.

As we explore these contrasts through the experience of living, we learn what Love is by feeling what it isn't, and within this lesson, we encounter suffering.

Suffering is not bad in and of itself and when seen as a tool. We awaken through suffering. Suffering not inflicted by God but us upon ourselves and each other, upon the animals, and upon the planet. Once suffering is experienced, we have a choice to either learn from it or deny its cause and *choose* to continue suffering. If we choose to continue with whatever is causing our suffering, it will blossom and morph into other forms of hardship and disease in an attempt to get our attention. It will become harder and harder to ignore, making us increasingly miserable until we reach a point life becomes impossible, literally. Game over.

The fact disease and suffering come from disconnection is not to imply a vindictive creative force; the creative and organizing force of all existence is Love beyond comprehension. Disease and suffering are not punishments but signposts or guiding forces pointing the way back to our hearts. Our bodies do not simply need oxygen, water, and food to survive. The force behind it all, divine Love, must be allowed to infiltrate and nourish every part of us. What animates the inanimate material from which you, I, and all life are made is this all-knowing, organizing force. When life is lived in wanton denial of truth; when judgment, hatred, and fear run rampant; the life affirming essence of this force is muted, the gift is rejected, ego dominates heart, and life's flow is impaired. Misery, suffering, and eventually disease will result.

Our Source is a respecter of laws, not of individuals. What this means is if you live within the divine law at the center of your being based on a loving and joyful compassion for life you will have a happy, fulfilling, and peaceful existence. Live a life of judgment, attachment, fear, defense, and anger, denying the force at the heart of your and all creation, and you may have a hard time. This is true regardless of what you might think God is. It is the energy of the thought and emotion with which you live your life, which is godlike or not, not your egoic and human opinions of what God is. It's not complicated, once your ego is surrendered. It is simply a matter of allowing.

Think of life as a strong current running one direction, like a river that is unstoppable. This river is Love. When we live in a way that goes with the flow, life is easy, just as it should be. The current carries us through the forever changing scenery of our lives, starting high in the mountains and emptying finally into the sea from which we came. When all is well, we can rest in the current, go at its pace, letting it take us where it will—always trusting it knows the way.

Ah, but maybe you are of the thinking you know the way better, that you have all the answers, that you are smart enough to go your own way and deny the force that animates your existence. Maybe swimming upstream and fighting the current makes more sense. Maybe you think you need something beyond what is already given, all which is already yours, and the only way you know how to do this is to fight for what you want—to struggle, to suffer … And so be it, you will. After all, you do get what you ask for in life. But my question would be this: how long do you think you can you swim? How long can you fight? How long will you struggle against what is completely and utterly unstoppable and intrinsic to all life throughout the Universe? Are you smarter than what created the oceans and all that lives within them? Are you smarter than life? Are you stronger than its flow?

Inevitably, even the strongest swimmer will grow tired, and if still resistant to the flow even after many years of opportunities to rest and learn, drowning may ensue, manifested as physical disease. Or maybe, through the pain and suffering inherent within the struggle, the lesson is learned that it is pointless to fight the current. Life becomes much more pleasant when one turns and simply floats along. The choice is yours; how long you want to fight life is completely up to you. Some learn the easy way, and some through immense suffering: drug addiction, chronic health conditions, the suffering of barbaric violence and tragedy. And some will never learn in this life.

It is a palpable sensation when one releases into the flow. You can actually sense the movement of the current, and the stars, moon, and tide never again look the same. You now realize their powerful perfection is your powerful perfection. Can you stop the tide? Can you keep the moon from rising? Neither can you stop the flow. It is bigger than you. And when one turns against the current as all humans will, the discomfort of doing so will be immediately recognized, the resistance will be palpable, and hopefully the correction is once again made. Life is an endless series of opportunities to choose the direction of your experience, either with the flow, relating to life through the heart, or against the flow, relating to life through resistance to what is, through the fearful material intellect. Accept or resist. Fight for what you think, or rest in what you *know*. Floating downstream with the current is natural. It is perfect, it is easy, and it is in line with natural law, which is why it feels so good.

Suffering results from resisting this flow. It emanates from belief and attachment. Suffering results from attachment to belief. The belief that we know what life is all about, that we know how it should be lived, by us and by everyone else, by thinking that ours is the best or only way.

The road to hell is paved with expectations.

We commonly make the mistake of thinking we know better than someone else how they should live or be. And this causes untold suffering for both parties. Families are torn apart by this simple mistake. Don't ever assume you know someone else's experience; you cannot. Every single person who has ever lived has had a unique experience and outlook resulting from it. The way I taste food is different from anyone else who has ever lived, the way the stars look, and what they mean to me is unique as well. I am the only one ever to gaze upon this world with these eyes, with this brain, and with this unique sensibility, and the same is true of all who have ever lived. We are all individual in the way we perceive and live our lives in every nuance, in every breath. We are each as unique as each snowflake. We are each eyeballs of what we call God itself, each seeing, feeling, and simply being in this exquisite concerto of divinity's making. And like a concerto, each instrument has its part, its place in the wonder of creation extending to every corner of every Universe, from now to beyond forever.

We cannot know what another has come here to learn and experience; we cannot know what another *has* experienced, what they feel in their hearts. We cannot know the internal dialogue they are having, the pain or joy they are concealing, the way they see themselves or their world.

Each of us is creating something unique in our experience, in our hearts and minds. Each truly dwells within a world of our own making, which lies beyond the bounds of human language to explain or describe. Our internal environment is ours alone to contemplate, and many of us don't even know how to do that. How can we know or judge someone else if we don't really know ourselves?

Our individuality is God given; it exists for a divine reason, and to judge others because they dare to be different or live differently or look differently is counter to this divine knowledge, which is why it causes so much pain.

This describes the roots of compassion. We are all doing the best we can with what we know right now. Some are very lost, at least according to outside eyes and opinions, but even the most desperate-appearing individuals are doing the best they can. But sometimes in their confusion, people suffer, often greatly.

The discordance and pain we live with every day is witness to this confusion.

Suffering comes from wanting things: money, better relationships, even happiness. But you cannot *get* happy; it is not something to be acquired. You can only *be* what you are beyond the limitations with which you have arbitrarily encumbered yourself. Pain, anger, and frustration will always follow when one becomes fixated on circumstance, when one attempts to micromanage life. Your heartbeat and breathing, and the myriad chemical and mechanical processes constantly at work to keep your body healthy and alive, require no conscious input from you. Neither does the rest of life. Take your hands off the wheel for a while and trust that what is spinning the Milky Way Galaxy is also taking care of you.

## Chapter 16

# Morning Glory

It's another fresh start, a new beginning, yet another chance at the game of life. What a gift. The Universe, every twenty-four hours, issues a do-over of sorts, and I sit here this morning holding my life in my hands. What am I going to do with it today?

I am the creator of my world. I am the creator of my experience. I can mold and shape, tweak and blend this day into what I want, at least in the realms of thought and feeling, and these things I use to explore and expand my world. This time and place is a most wonderful canvas. What colors will I use today? How will I frame it?

My heart and eyes are open; I am alive for a reason. There is always a choice. Will I fall into another mindless rut, or will I soar? Will I live in appreciation of the gift that is this day, or will I sleep through it again? Will I notice the caress of the afternoon breeze as it gently stirs the hair on my arms? Will I take the time to feel all that is held within the sun's warmth or be happily transfixed by the grace of a passing bird? Or will I allow these things and the many others which color my experience to pass by unnoticed?

Today I vow to let myself honestly feel my joy *and* my pain. I vow to use life's frustrations and challenges to lift and move me farther down my path, all the while carrying the knowledge they are wonderful opportunities to practice what I already know. Inherent in this, a deep knowing persists that all struggles will pass as surely as the mist at dawn, leaving me with only the priceless gift of having grown due to their presence.

In the ongoing healing process that is life, every breath is another opportunity to reconnect with what is real, every trauma an opportunity to heal myself and my world through the act of loving with an open heart, because there is no other way to truly heal—or truly see. I am a reflection of the life I've lived and the life I've loved, all of it. It is what I am, it is what I do, it is why I am here, and I share it freely with the world.

I give thanks for these lungs that breathe, this heart that beats, and the heart that loves. I give thanks for eyes that see, ears that hear, and legs which move me through my world. I give thanks to all who have touched my life. Those who have lingered, and those who shimmered and flashed ever so brightly while streaking across my life like a shooting star, I love you all.

Today, I will see love reflected in the smile of a stranger. I will be aware of the nourishing air behind the leaves' subtle whisper. I will bless the quenching water as it gently kisses the shore. I will merge with the warm light which gives rise to all; I will *be* the flowers' brilliance. I will cry, I will smile, I will laugh, and I will strive to love myself and my world completely as I let myself deeply feel all I am, was, and will ever be. Today, I will simply listen.

## Chapter 17

## Chemical Craziness

Depression is real, or so they say. And I would have to agree, to a point. The commercials say there are real reasons for it, chemical imbalances or something like that. I don't really need to know because the people in white coats with alphabets after their names are telling me this, so it must be true. After all, they're *experts*.

There are so many examples—fibromyalgia, depression, gout, and many more—maladies with TV commercials purporting miracle treatments promising a better life for those suffering their ills.

I was diagnosed with depression in 2001. Of course, it was an entirely erroneous diagnosis, and I now disagree with it vehemently, but I want it known that I have suffered the symptoms of what is termed depression, as many people have. I also deeply feel that what is commonly diagnosed as depression is nothing but a response of a heart that has chronically suffered the attacks of the mind; it is emblematic of how we live, inevitable really. It is an issue of Love's denial at the hands of judgment.

In late 2001, right after the September 11 attacks, I was overcome by a feeling of despondent hopelessness. I had just relocated to Alaska, thousands of miles from all I knew, I was working in a hospital doing a job I hated, and I was suffering from debilitating chronic neck pain. When 9/11 occurred, it was the proverbial straw that broke the camel's back. I had been suffering the signs of depression for years for various reasons that have been discussed throughout this book, but like so many, I plodded along, thinking that feeling this way was somehow normal but *knowing* somewhere deep it was not. When the senselessness of that day played out before me and most of humanity, I suddenly felt a sadness that transcended what I considered to be the normal sadness of everyday life. It wasn't anger I felt like so many seemed to. It wasn't fear. It was a deep spiritual sadness. A sadness that spoke to our essential condition, to a mourning felt so deeply for where we had fallen as a species.

In 2007, during my course of craniosacral treatments, I wrote the following when I had an "aha" moment regarding my depression. I had worked in emergency medicine for years and I enjoyed it. I had no idea the toll it was taking on my spirit along with all of my chronic pain. I had the sudden insight that much of what I thought was depression was the proper response to seeing firsthand the desecration of life.

At the tender and relatively innocent age of nineteen, I watched my best friend lie on the side of the road twitching and bleeding to death after a rollover car accident. Want to talk about helplessness? Want to talk about shock, profound sadness, and utter emotional devastation? Want to talk about mental images and feelings which will never leave my memory? And what's more, it wasn't dealt with appropriately, or really at all.

Then, for reasons I scarcely understood at the time, I become an EMT and spent many years witnessing more and more of the ridiculous and savage side of human nature. I experienced the senseless acts of wanton violence perpetrated by one human against another, the profound and hopeless destitution of the homeless, the bleak desperation of abject poverty, and the seemingly random and unfair acts of accidental tragedy.

Every day I was submerged into this world ... *for years*. Then I went to work in a trauma center, where the human suffering was even further concentrated and on sublime display. I can still smell the blood.

I actually enjoyed the work at the time. It was exciting and varied and rarely boring, but what

I didn't realize was that it was taking a spiritual toll. While most people in this line of work have tough and resilient protective barriers by necessity, I now realize there was part of me, a very elemental, important, and sensitive part, which I was unable to protect. And that part was injured a little bit by every sad story, by every injustice, by every tragedy. I remember internalizing the frustration regarding the utter senselessness of what I saw. Most of the suffering simply did not need to happen, but these people, through whatever mechanisms, were destroying themselves and each other (and, it turns out, me). And for what? It could not be understood.

But the straw which really broke my spirit's back was 9/11. I, like every good American, was devastated by the senseless brutality of that day. I remember seeking help for depression in the weeks following, and in typical American medical fashion, my doctor just threw pills at the problem. In his defense, what else could he do? But nonetheless, I was not helped and I was not able to find help, so this pain was just shoved down into the little storehouse of horrors within my soul for safekeeping. And I continued to spiral out of control physically and psychically as the weight of all this unresolved pain, frustration, and emotion began to crush me from within.

At the time, I was not a student of the human heart, or of Love. And I was a numb. I was an average middle-class American, naïve perhaps, but to me 9/11 was not a national issue, an American issue—it was a human issue. The questions bounced around: how could a small group of people kill thousands of innocent men, women, and children in one unbelievably barbaric moment, and further, how could they do so in the name of God? I was stunned by how cold, heartless and hateful we humans can be. I didn't understand then that such a ruthless and heartless act was a sign of a larger issue, a symptom of greater disease that has nothing to do with God. In fact, things like that can only occur within a profound dearth of understanding of the essential nature of Love, God, and life itself. The pain I experienced that day, and that many others experienced, was one that lies far beyond everyday human experience. It was the pain suffered by our collective heart when we as a species do something so counter to our nature and the nature of our Creator that it leaves us breathless with confusion and pain.

So I was depressed, and I didn't like being so. I felt helpless in my suffering, so I did what we are taught to do when we hurt: I went to the doctor and got some pills.

Please understand the following in an indictment of how we treat so-called "disease" in this country as a whole. It is not an attack on the innocent and trusting people who are suffering and who trust medical science to have the answers. It is written from the perspective of someone who beat depression completely. I know what happened to me works beyond any and all need for validation or approval from anyone, least of all medical science. I know this simply because I experienced it—because *I did it*. Period. I believe I know from where depression comes because I have been there, and I particularly know from where it comes because now I live its polar opposite. I know from where it comes because *I live precisely what it is not*. I assure you the peace I feel is unwavering.

That said, if you take medication for depression, please do not stop it abruptly or without a doctor's care; that can be dangerous. Please just let this missive open the doors to what I hope could be a greater understanding of something that is nearly epidemic in this country.

I also want to say that at times, I feel medication has a place. If the issue at hand cannot be handled any other way, if the person is not ready to approach it another way, if someone is in an acute state of suffering, medication and conventional medicine can help. And that is a good thing as long as it is seen for what it is—a temporary treatment, not a cure.

I write this to say what I feel needs to be said, things many are afraid to acknowledge, that depression and many other "diseases" are our responsibility. We create them, and we can cure them. Medical science would have us believe that we are innocent victims of faulty machinery, but this is rarely, if ever, the case. I am trying to help those who are suffering because I was one of them and I found my way out of the woods. I want to honor my fellow humans who are struggling by helping them see they are much more than our medical system would indulge or can even acknowledge, with the way it is currently practiced and with the way the system is set up. To treat something as spiritually significant as depression and many other maladies by simply writing something on a piece of paper is not honoring the whole of the person; it is not honoring the person at all. We are not simply machines with individuated parts which are to be tinkered with in specific isolation like those of a broken down car. Nothing, including depression occurs in a vacuum.

Studies have shown there is a chemical imbalance in the brains of people who suffer from depression. The shortsighted among us or those who have put financial motives ahead of compassion have assumed and proclaimed this imbalance is the *cause* of the issue; what I feel is a rather rudimentary correlation at best. Accepting the fact a deficiency of serotonin is present in the brains of those who are depressed, shouldn't the next question be: what is causing the imbalance? You'd think this would be obvious, but it doesn't seem to be as the line of inquiry seems to stop here. Either by design or through ignorance, the *assumption* is made that abnormal serotonin, norepinephrine, or dopamine levels, or whatever the substance de jour is at the time, must be the problem. Therefore, the treatment is, of course, aimed at correcting the imbalance. It makes sense in a shallow, shortsighted, and superficial sort of way.

This is, of course, the easiest and most profitable answer. The drug companies can then bottle a proprietary blend of toxic chemicals they don't know all that much about, patent it, give it a cute name, make a TV commercial, charge an exorbitant amount of money for the promise of a brighter tomorrow contained within a magical little brown bottle, and then we will all be happy!

But consider this for a moment: is there a possibility the clinically noted relationship of neurotransmitter imbalance and the signs and symptoms of depression is but a tiny part of the overall picture? Could it be the chemical imbalance is simply another manifestation, another symptom of a greater issue? Of course, it is. The fact that such a simple feat of logic is not available to those with white coats and alphabets after their names in puzzling. Do the drug companies really believe what they parrot, or is there some other motive for their overt simplicity?

Displaying such a lack of understanding of the concept of causation is once again prolonging pain and suffering and perhaps even causing it. Inserting or forcing intervention at the wrong point in an inherently complex causative chain, especially when that intervention involves powerful, toxic chemicals with unknown mechanisms and significant side effects, is at best irresponsible.

Like most medical issues, depression is spiritually based. But perhaps depression feels more so due to the proximity of the constellation of symptoms to what we hold inherently as sacred, essential, and intuitively close to the center of our experience. Depression is a spiritual crisis.

There is no doubt depression can be debilitating. It steals the flavor from one's existence; it dulls the senses and disallows what is inherently ours *by the very fact of our existence*—joy, contentment, and the wellspring of everything—Love. Depression results from the severing of the umbilical cord of life, pinching off its divine flow, thereby insulating one from the subtleties of life's nuance, beauty, and grace. It fools one into thinking there is no point to existence, to life, that there is no reason to try or be. Depression results from an error in thinking resulting in the illusion one is separate, alone, unloved, and without purpose. It is the result of forgetting who and what we are and how we are forever connected and inseparable from our divine nature. It results from the overemphasis of the importance of the trivial, at the cost of neglecting an acknowledgment and honoring of the essential, all the while giving far too much importance to the illusion of time. It arises from the notion the circumstances of one's life are not what they ought to be, and the resultant frustration inherent in fighting a battle against what cannot be fought. Some might call this resistance.

Ultimately, depression results from egoic judgment, inducing a perceived disconnection from or doubting of Source, what created you and trillions of suns. How could you *ever* doubt this connection? And don't you think it may hurt a bit when you do? When this most essential of facts, the one which is beyond all appearances and beyond all thought, that which lies at the heart of *everything*, is denied, don't you think your emotional system may try to make the error known? When you live unaware of the larger picture, of your larger essence, unaware of even the presence of the sacred mystery, denying the intelligence which causes the sun to shine and the waves to crash upon the shore, denying your own grandeur, make no mistake: you will suffer. How could you not?

But suffering of this nature is not a bad thing. Depression should be seen as an opportunity for spiritual advancement, a sign that something needs changing. Like everything else, it *always* has a reason, a reason that needs to be heeded, explored, honored, and processed, and a reason I feel should not to be trivialized by the act of taking a pill. My God, how ridiculous are we to think that such an issue can be dealt with in such a way? It borders on the obscene.

How we approach this issue and many others is a symptom of how backward we really are. We worship at the altar of numbers, attempting to measure the immeasurable, smugly certain and naïvely arrogant. As long as phenomena fit into an arbitrary box which can be validated by known methods and means, we deem it as *real*. All else is minimalized, ignored, and dismissed. We expect the intellectual mind to solve problems itself has created through its ignorance and confusion. And worse, we look to *other* intellectual minds, those who do not necessarily have our best interests at heart, to solve the problems that we are here to work out for ourselves in a more organic fashion, for reasons much deeper than we usually now. We look for mechanical solutions for non-mechanical issues, defined by a narrow and cold empiricism for things that will always defy such pedantic categorization, things that lie far beyond our ability to perceive utilizing our simple, primitive, naïve, and foolish investigations.

The egoic mind, the illusions it perpetrates, and the judgments it holds are the real cause of depression. If you are depressed, I would ask this: where in your life are you holding judgment against yourself, others, or society? Where are you judging things aren't the way they are *supposed* to be? Where do you hold the idea you are not good enough, pretty enough, thin enough, or rich enough? What past actions or mistakes are you still holding onto with a guilt that stings, a regret that burns? What memories tumble out of the dark in the middle of the night without invitation, incessantly playing over and over in the theater of your mind, twisting your gut into knots? What are you worrying about when sitting in traffic, mind racing, teeth unconsciously clenched, while that vague and always present anxiety and dissatisfaction roil just under the surface? Where do you feel empty and disconnected, helpless or disempowered? What lies do you hold that justify all that pain? Notice that all these things exist either in the past or in the future; they are imaginings or projections. Therefore, *they are not real*; your higher self knows this and is screaming at you the only way it can—by making you feel *bad* and forcing you to take notice. I would have to ask. Where else are you denying the present moment?

It needs to be pointed out that *every single one* of the things written above is caused by the ego and its denial of the perfect divine love of which you are, without exception.

These thoughts and feelings, when indulged incessantly over time, will wreak havoc throughout the body, mind, and heart, and no pill is going to stop it. It begins with depression, but it can and will progress to virtually all other so-called "diseases" that are epidemic in the modern world. Which one will manifest in any particular person is as varied as people are. Anxiety in all its forms, gastrointestinal disorders of all forms, addiction, fibromyalgia, and other forms of idiopathic or autoimmune disorders—it goes on and on. And then, when all else is denied and ignored, looms the most intimidating and feared teacher of all: cancer. The commonality is the way all these maladies are treated by our medical system, treating effect rather than cause. Unfortunately, *all these "diseases" are effects, not causes, in and of themselves.* When a TV commercial states, "The root cause of gout is high uric acid," it is misinformed, to say the least. The *root* cause of gout is whatever is *causing* the high uric acid; the high uric acid is as much a symptom as the pain. *It is not the cause.* When we commonly, wantonly, and perhaps even intentionally mistake symptoms for causes at the highest levels of medical science, we are indeed lost.

Depression particularly is a spiritual conundrum. It lies at the heart of why we are here. It is a reminder of what we are to overcome and remember. It screams of self-judgment and disconnection. It screams of the ego being in charge. It screams of resistance. The question must be asked: does depression serve to disconnect or does disconnection serve to depress? My vote is for the latter; medical science seems to vote for the former. The difference is responsibility. Who wouldn't rather take a pill than to face the pain in their heart? And the modern medical system, whether by design or not, is complicit. The thing making the depressed miserable is very cunning, powerful, and fearful of being made irrelevant. It does not go away with the act of taking medication, *and it never will*. It only goes away with the surrender of all opinion, control, judgment, and fear. These are but four different faces of the same coin, and are all intertwined; they will fall like dominoes when the light of truth is shined upon them.

A friend, a mental health worker, once asked me "How does this apply to depressed or sick kids? They haven't had the time to learn how to become depressed like adults, and to suffer other forms of self-created disease."

This is my letter back to her:

> How can we know the joy of the light without experiencing the pain of the dark? Depression is about what we are here for … to feel the contrast between connection and disconnection, light and dark, ego and heart, acceptance and resistance, Love and anything that isn't Love … All this is but one duality expressed many different ways. Depression gives joy context … A pill is never going help someone actually overcome the dark. Now, it may help some people feel better so they can function and perhaps stem the suffering a little, and that is okay by me, especially in the short term. It is when there are TV ads telling me that it isn't my fault, all I have to do is buy this chemical, and everything is going to be okay, that steam tends to come out of my ears. It is

such a disservice to the person, most of whom implicitly trust the medical system.

I was asked about sick kids by a client once who was a pediatric oncology nurse. Talk about an emotionally draining job if you aren't in tip-top emotional shape. She said she had an idea why adults might get cancer, but why do little ones?

An answer came with hands still on her ... I told her that I think there are many reasons for what appears to be suffering. One, a soul may choose to manifest with what most would consider to be limitations. Down syndrome, autism, birth defects, etc. teach not only the ones with the issue but also all those around them, and society, that Love can always be found. They do this by challenging people to love unconditionally, regardless of the struggle or dysfunction or outward appearance, thereby teaching Love is all that matters and that indeed it does conquer all. The limitation, what we judge as the less-than-ideal body or mind, is seen first as an obstacle but then as something as worthy of Love as anything or anybody who is "normal," while at the same time it is realized through this process the body and intellectual mind are indeed irrelevant in the higher planes to which we all aspire. A sick child who passes on teaches the pain of loss and all its attendant lessons, that we need to feel hopeless, sad, and overwhelmed so that we may learn the glory of their opposites—joy, happiness, and love. By doing this, hopefully the realization is made there is no death, that even attachment to this body and this life is false and in reality impossible, and that much pain ensues when this is disregarded. Nothing is permanent. We may learn that even our children aren't really ours and that all souls choose when they leave *without exception,* and to accept this is indeed a powerful lesson of letting go, even when the letting go is of a child, which may be the most difficult emotional trauma a human being can face.

With depression, who is to say that a young person isn't as spiritually mature as you or me? Who is to say what some of us come into this life already carrying? Perhaps the depressed kid is sensitive to all the unhealthy vibration around him not only in the house where he may live but also in the world at large. Depression can sometimes be a very accurate response to madness. What about the pre-birth environment? I feel that if a child is conceived without love, gestated in an environment of fear, and raised in an environment where basic needs are denied, with Love being the most basic of those needs, then a baby begins life already fractured, already behind the eight ball, and sentenced to a life of struggle very early. It could be a lot of things, but I do know that man-made neurotransmitter modulation will not cure it. It may treat it, and that may be necessary, but it will take digging a little deeper to actually find a cause and thus a meaningful way out.

Release from much of the suffering regarding disease comes from acknowledging responsibility, and this is not to imply guilt. We need to know how to acknowledge responsibility without jumping to judgment. We can be completely responsible for something without being guilty of anything. The ego doesn't understand this, but part of us must. When we accept responsibility and understand cause, we can transform illness into something positive: learning.

When we distance ourselves from our issues and detach from our identification with them, they lose much of their power to create havoc.

Suffering for years from neck pain ostensibly caused by multiple cervical disc extrusions induced by physical trauma, I had the sensibility of, and had unknowingly embraced, the role of victim. Something happened *to* me beyond my control. I suffered an insult to my body and I hurt, so now I embraced willingly the part of "sufferer." What else could I do? It is not that I wasn't in a serious car accident as a teen. I was. And it wasn't that I felt every bit of the pain over those dark, lonely years. I surely did. I've seen the MRIs with my own eyes. I've read the reports. I've talked to countless doctors, chiropractors, and physical therapists, and there is no doubt the injuries and the deformities are there. But the pain that was previously attributed to them is not. Could it be that years of chronic muscle tension caused by spiritual/emotional factors actually created, or at the very least exacerbated, the spinal issues? I routinely suffered muscle spasms that would wrench me to my knees, laying me out for days. The power of my own body, of my own muscles, was profound, even frightening, and the pain created was unbearable. I now have no doubt those years of emotionally induced, abnormal muscle tension pulled the vertebrae out of alignment chronically, eventually deforming the tissue into a clinically significant, verifiable, and diagnosable issue. Emotion caused the physical injury every bit as much as physical injury caused the depressive emotion. The pain was a result of not listening, even though my body was screaming at me.

We treat symptoms while ignoring cause with glaring regularity. Do you suffer from heartburn? Here, take a pill to neutralize the acid rather than attempt to understand why the indigestion is occurring, which could very well be emotionally based (i.e., chronic anger and/or anxiety). By taking a pill, we are missing an opportunity to learn.

Do you clench your teeth at night? Here, put this rubber guard in your mouth and never mind the emotional angst, usually frustration, which is often the real cause of what is known as *bruxism*.

Can't sleep, huh? Here, take this powerful pill that will change the actual chemistry of your brain in ways that even the manufacturer admittedly doesn't completely understand, instead of dealing with what usually causes sleeplessness: runaway egoic thought.

Do you suffer from gout? Take this pill to modulate the metabolism of uric acid instead of taking gout as a sign that you are eating or doing something your body does not want or need. It could be as simple as dehydration. Think of that big toe as a sentinel telling you there is an imbalance, and then heed it. Your body is talking to you.

Linda was a client I had who suffered from ulcerative colitis (UC). She had had it for years and had tried all the treatments—steroids, altered diet, aspirin-based suppositories—all to no avail. After years of suffering, she agreed to be put on an immunosuppressant, a drug usually used to treat post-transplant organ rejection, a use for which it is completely appropriate. This incredibly powerful and destructive drug works by knocking out certain components of the immune system, thereby decreasing the inflammatory response believed to be at the heart of UC. And by all accounts, it does work. It does decrease the symptoms experienced by those suffering from this particular malady. But at what cost?

Your immune system is a miracle of intelligence dwelling within your body. It has consciousness; it has developed over immense amounts of time with intelligence beyond our comprehension to do what it does, and it does so perfectly. It does not go haywire for no reason. Knocking it out is like burning down the house to get rid of mice in the attic. And Linda learned this the hard way by developing a serious infection due to use of the drug which required more than a week in the hospital and a long course of treatment with powerful and very expensive antibiotics. It turns out this was a sentinel event for her, and it could be seen as a life-saving event because if her immune system has been sufficiently attenuated to the point of allowing such an infection in an otherwise healthy woman, it had been lowered to a point which cancer becomes a very real possibility. Luckily, Linda heeded the warning given by her body and stopped taking the drug.

When she got on my treatment table, I was immediately drawn to her belly. After some discussion, we discovered she had been holding onto a great amount of fear in that area regarding her childhood. Her father was a very stern and threatening man whom she feared, and this set up as tension representing chronic worry and self-deprecation in her GI tract. She grew up regularly being told she wasn't good enough at whatever it was she tried to do. Always criticized and never feeling accepted, she was never praised when she did do something well, and through this she was taught at a tender age that she wasn't worthy of love. Of course, this also led to depression. During therapy, she made the connection that her gut issues became worse when her stress became worse, and when she engaged in fearful or toxic thinking regarding whatever was going on in her life. She realized that she was still fighting for acceptance: from her family, friends and co-workers. But most importantly, she was fighting to accept herself.

She realized that her "inner voice" was constantly berating her; it was like a little tyrannical judge between her ears who criticized her without mercy, telling her she needed to work harder and be better at everything she did. Even though she was an intelligent, successful and beautiful woman, her voice told her she was ugly, and that she wasn't smart. She then had the insight that her belly was trying to tell her something. It told her it needed Love, that *she* needed Love; it needed her to pay attention to the character of her thoughts, to stop abusing herself. In tears, she released much of the tension she carried in her abdomen, and she forgave her now deceased father and herself and promised to work on the chronic and self-abusive self-talk that she engaged in as a matter of habit.

And guess what? Her symptoms all but disappeared within a week. This was confirmed by, much to her GI doc's surprise, the fact there was no evidence of active inflammatory processes in her colon, as verified by colonoscopy several months later.

I tell this story not to claim that craniosacral therapy cures ulcerative colitis or anything else. I tell it to elucidate the fact that we can heal ourselves with proper self-awareness. And for this sometimes we need external guidance. But you are the only one that can truly heal you. An issue put there by the mind can be removed by the mind. Self-knowledge and honesty are often the keys to accessing the real causes of disease.

How much money, how much suffering, and how much time is wasted because we don't acknowledge the more ethereal and primary causes of much of what we call disease? In all her visits to specialists regarding this issue, the word *stress* was never discussed. It was egoic fear ultimately which caused years of suffering for Linda. The fear caused stress as all fear does, causing a chronic sub-acute fight or flight reaction within her body. This released hormones that had a deleterious effect on her GI tract, a part of the body richly innervated by the sympathetic nervous system that is in charge of "fight or flight". Remember, the body knows no difference between real and imagined threats. Fear is fear, and the body always reacts *perfectly* to it. Unfortunately, it is the mind that keeps sounding what is in reality a false alarm.

As said many times, the ego-fear-stress trinity lies at the heart of many chronic ailments we suffer in modern life. Heart disease, stroke, hypertension, GI issues, and anxiety—it goes on and on. And by now, we should have made the connection that stress comes from one place alone, and that is egoic fear. It can be said that ego-generated fear is the cause of nearly all human suffering in one way or another.

Chronic fear-related stress decreases the efficacy of the immune system, so further diminishment of it via medication was the last thing Linda needed. And this weakening of the immune system over time can allow cancer to take hold, because the body is always manufacturing cancer cells. The drug she took is classified as a group 1 carcinogen, meaning it *causes cancer in humans*. It isn't simply suspected of doing so, it does. It is also classified as "cytotoxic" meaning it is toxic to cells (cyto = cell), in fact, that is exactly how it works: by destroying *healthy* immune cells. Do you think her doctor explained this to her fully? Would you put this into your body if you knew what it really was?

It seems that modern medicine is at the precarious place of knowing just enough to be dangerous. By fooling with chemicals like this and giving them to entirely unsuspecting and trusting people who are for the most part ignorant of what it is they are putting in their bodies, much suffering is created, not alleviated.

It is a most amazing thing, the immune system. It is by far the greatest preventer of cancer there is or ever could be; nothing created in a lab or ingested through the mouth can even come close. Keeping it healthy by engaging in life-affirming and loving thoughts is the best possible defense against cancer, and why wouldn't that be? Aligning yourself with the power and intelligence of your manufacturer, so to speak, is what has the most power to keep you truly healthy. There is no truer power.

Medical science is finally making some of these connections. In a study reported by Scientific American, dated February 11, 2011, entitled- *Neurostress: How Stress May Fuel Neurodegenerative Diseases*, researchers linked stress with the occurrence of Alzheimer's disease, which is not really a shock. The thinking is that the hormones released due to stress can adversely affect the number of synapses present in the brain, which can affect how brain cells communicate. I am sure it won't be long until drug companies attempt to find a way to use this information to develop drugs that will interfere with the effects of stress hormones on brain tissue. But here's an idea. What if we, instead of developing yet another drug, simply learn how to exist and live with less stress? We seem to accept chronic stress is somehow a normal part of life. Why? Where is that written? Why don't we make an effort to learn that most stress is unnecessary, self-imposed, and false?

The article goes on to say that heredity also seems to play a factor in the development of Alzheimer's disease. But could it be that the likelihood of the disease is not genetically predetermined as such (i.e., to be found on the genome) but that its presence is indicative of the *learned* fear one lives with, something we picked up from our parents, which could be said to be hereditary in its own way? Could it be that we are destined to follow the same path of disease and illness they have not because of something to be found in our DNA but because we live and approach life like they did, with either Love and patience or worry and fear? Could it be that a correlation is erroneously made that genetics is responsible when in effect it is learned behavior related to the person's familial environment and upbringing? Could it be that much of this very expensive and complicated research into disease, using the latest in super science and genetics, is often unnecessary? Could it be that if we live peaceful, loving, and accepting lives where the real causes of stress are controlled and even ameliorated, is all we need to stay healthy for a very long time? Could health and wellness be this simple?

I think the answer is a resounding yes.

But this again speaks to the egoic nature of our society. When we try to micromanage our health by dissecting it into smaller and smaller pieces, we miss the point of what health really is. False correlations are then easily made.

Another study called The Amsterdam Study of the Elderly (Amstel), has found a correlation between loneliness and an increased likelihood of Alzheimer's disease. Study participants who were "lonely" were found to be twice as likely to develop Alzheimer's and other forms of dementia as those who were not. The study did distinguish loneliness from simply being alone, and this is good because there is a huge difference. As harsh as it may sound, loneliness is a self-imposed, egoic judgment based on the desire for things to be different than they are, and it ultimately arises from fear. Therefore, by definition, it is a stressful state. And we just learned what stress can do to brain tissue. Being alone can be lonely or it can be a completely comfortable, wonderful, and enriching experience. That judgment is completely up to the person, and so are the consequences.

Which speaks again to responsibility. We are taught that to be responsible, we need to eat well, cut out the fat and salt, and get exercise. But we are not taught that the most powerful determining factor regarding our health is how we think. We are never taught that the only thing in this life we can truly control is our thoughts. We are never taught that we have a responsibility to ourselves, the people we love, and all of humanity to think correctly, which means lovingly. All we manifest in our lives comes from thought, every bit of it—all our health, all our joy, all our misery, all our pain, and all our material abundance. Everything comes from our thoughts. The hell on earth we have created was created entirely with our thoughts.

Why don't we think about that for a minute?

Thoughts are the only thing we can control. This bears repeating. *Thoughts are the only thing we can control.* All else in our experience is a consequence of thought. It is madness to believe we can control the outcomes in our life without first controlling thought.

For whatever reason, rampant, wild, and destructive thought is tolerated by us as something that is uncontrollable and unavoidable. When we lie awake at night, prisoners of our fearful and worrisome thoughts, what can we do but lie there and take it? We can take a pill and attempt to hide, but when those chronic thoughts manifest as anxiety and depression, we are told it is not our fault and that it is simply the body going wrong.

Depression is reflective of the ego's regret about the past, and anxiety is reflective of the ego's fear of the future. We are far too accepting of the mind's wandering; we are far too tolerant of the pain that is caused by it.

So much of our suffering comes from ourselves; so much pain arises from our judgments. We are not as gentle with ourselves as we should be. We are not tolerant of our mistakes and perceived shortcomings. We are as quick to judge and persecute ourselves as we are each other, and maybe quicker because we think we do it in secret. There is no social stigma involved with toxic self-talk. We think there are no ramifications in attacking ourselves with a violence we wouldn't wish on anyone else.

From my journal ...

> How much of my neck pain was due to psychically induced tension, the result of poisonous thought? Once again, I am surprised and startled by the

truth and beauty of the mind-body interface, and it's become exquisitely obvious that the ethereal realm of thought, feeling, and emotion can and does infiltrate flesh and bone and will impart effect, either deleterious or salutary depending upon the character of the thought or feeling.

Through focused introspection and the ensuing insight, I had already come to the conclusion that I needed some work in regards to how I treat myself. My inner dialogue has been for a long time one of constant abuse. Shame, anger, frustration, disgust, and regret were the words that defined my inner vocabulary, and subsequently these words defined *me*. I realized that every few minutes on average for the last thirty years I had unleashed their dark power and had been harmed by their poison, and every time a little part of me, the real me, died. This was manifested physically in many forms, and not surprisingly, all were negative in nature.

I didn't consciously realize and understand the gravity and totality of its effect on every aspect of my life, and only recently have I become painfully aware of the internal hate speech with which I constantly berate myself. This is not productive and healthy; in fact, it is profoundly counterproductive, toxic, and ultimately destructive to the life force itself. The question needs to be asked: why do I abuse myself like this? I wouldn't ever consider treating another human being so maliciously, so why would I do it to myself? Where did I learn this?

And in this lies a grand lesson. Love begins within. It cannot be extended until it is known, it cannot be shared until it allowed, and it also illuminates that we *learn* how to destroy ourselves with this kind of internal warfare, and therein lies the secret to liberation. If it can be learned, *it can be unlearned.*

It should be apparent now that all healing comes from within. All true healing is spiritual healing which is to be made whole again. The body will follow. It is the undoing of the errors that have caused you to fracture and become separate within yourself. It is the reparation of your being.

Being in a connected and loving state of awareness is infinitely more impactful on our health than anything we can do outside of ourselves with regards to what we call "wellness." Our bodies were created by, and thrive on, loving energy; it is our most essential "food." It makes sense that what created us is what sustains us and is ultimately what keeps us healthy; the cutting off of that loving, nourishing flow through engaging chronically in thoughts and actions which enable fear and deny Love will take its toll physically.

We forget this because we don't see Love; we can't pick it up and touch it. We can't go to the store and buy it, cook it, and eat it. We also miss this most essential of facts because we are never told of it by those we trust with our health—because there is no money in it. It defies scientific analysis; therefore, it cannot be externally controlled. You can't patent Love, you can't bottle it, nor can it be prescribed.

Loving energy given freely by the Universe is what organizes us, energizes us, enlivens us, and heals us. Health is an ongoing process. It is not a state that is attained or lost; it simply is. Every moment is another chance to allow it or not. It is up to you. It is not measured by how far you can run or how many push-ups you can do; it cannot be reflected in laboratory values. It is not something that can be manipulated, forced, or attained by taking any kind of pill, prescription or otherwise. Health is a reflection of consciousness. Whether it is allowed or not is the question. Where it is denied, limited, or blocked through chronic thoughts of anger, worry, or fear, illness and dysfunction will result. We are essentially disconnected from the very source of life.

Your cells know nothing other than now. When the language of now, otherwise known as truth, is disallowed by constant distraction from it, or when one is living in or regretting the past, or focused upon or worried about the future, cells suffer. And when cells suffer, the organism suffers.

Our bodies are forever talking to us and the voice is there for us to hear if we choose to listen. Our bodies will educate us as to where we may be going astray. My body let me know of my errors with profound physical pain, primarily in my neck. Yes, as stated before, I have clinically diagnosed cervical disc issues and fairly serious ones at that, but the pain I felt in my neck and shoulders for over twenty years was completely erased with the gaining of knowledge about the higher truths and the letting go of all that was false. The miracle is that when I relinquished incessant thinking with present-moment awareness, my pain disappeared. When I surrendered all that never was and could never be, my pain disappeared. When I let go of all that was false, my pain disappeared. When I paid attention to my life, my emotional state, how I felt inside and out, when I took the time to let myself feel and then explore those feelings, my pain disappeared. When I dropped constant intellectual neediness for heart-centered openness, my pain disappeared.

Our bodies have many ways of speaking. Jaw clenching, tight shoulders, heartburn, fatigue, sleeplessness, anxiety, and depression are messages from our bodies that something is not quite right on the inside. And what do we usually do with the gift, this wealth of information that exists to help us be happy, healthy, and grow? We squash it with distraction, drugs, and therapies prescribed by doctors and prescribed by ourselves. We avoid what is causing the issue at all costs while treating the symptoms alone.

This comes from mistaking what the body really is.

We think the body is us because the ego thinks it is the body. The body and the ego are the two things that came into this physical life together, and they are the two things that will eventually die. Of course, the real you does not die, cannot die, and is not vulnerable to anything, but the ego and body do not know this. They *are* vulnerable. The ego and the body are tied in vulnerability; they are vulnerable to violence, injury, and attack; and they are susceptible to death. The body is often more of a hostage really, if the ego has commandeered it to do its bidding, but we can change this. The body can be liberated by awareness.

Freedom arises when we view the body differently. We commonly see it as a machine made up of various parts that are somehow separate, and we attempt to dispel the fear of losing it and its functionality by micromanaging our health. But if we widen our definition of what our body is and we maintain a loving but detached view of its real purpose, we can free ourselves of the need to obsess about our health. And by so doing, we will actually become healthier and more alive.

First, the body is a vehicle for the spirit to inhabit—a rental car if you will—to be used for the purpose of getting around and experiencing physical life on this planet. Secondly, it is a means of communication between spirits for the purpose of learning what we came here to learn. And thirdly, it is a guidance system for keeping ourselves on track via emotion, sensation, and the relative presence or absence of wellness or disease.

In a nutshell, the body is a place for the development of the spirit. It tells us in many ways if we are learning correctly. When we are off track, we feel it as bad or uncomfortable emotion and then disease. When we are on track, we feel it as health, joy, Love and even bliss.

The body creates pain each time we subject it to unloving thought. Anger, sadness, and fear are some of the effects of thoughts of this nature. They will accumulate in the tissue, wreaking havoc until they are dealt with, learned from, reconciled, and released.

Put simply, all emotion that feels bad arises from fear; all that feels good arises from Love. This awareness is a gift you have been given to stay on the path to where you want to be.

If we continue to live in a way that accepts and tolerates emotion that doesn't feel good, and we do it habitually and chronically, dysfunction, disease and even death will result.

This is because Love, given freely by the Universe, is what holds us together. If it is disallowed, the organism will move toward disintegration and chaos rather than integration and unity. The tendency toward chaos is reflected in disease; it is the disintegration of the physical you.

Love integrates—fear disintegrates.

Thought resonates vibrationally throughout the body; it penetrates and affects every single cell. Loving thought equates with health; unloving thought equates with disease.

Put another way ... *Every loving thought nourishes; every unloving one punishes.*

Now we can see how negatively thinking and disallowing the nourishing and organizing force we call Love can lead to all kinds of disease, including cancer. And this explains why, with all the science and with all the economic might brought to bear by laboratories and pharmaceutical companies all over the world, with the financial support of all the fundraisers and foundations, we have not found or even come close to finding a true cure for cancer. And as harsh as it sounds, because they are not looking in the right place, I don't think they ever will.

As simplistic and naïve as it may sound to some, the answer to cancer lies within our hearts.

And to me, this is no surprise. We already have everything we need to be healthy because it all comes from within. The body, due to the nature of its origin, is infinitely creative and intelligent. Why would the intelligence behind our creation and millions of years of evolution create an organism that suddenly needs specialized care to survive? It is no coincidence that the most profound healing experience of my life and the most profound healing I have witnessed in others has come from nothing but a pair of open, loving, and sensitive hands. It is no coincidence that what created us gave us all we need to heal.

And that may be the most beautiful realization of all.

## Chapter 18

## *Passages*

What does it all mean?

It means life is about choice. Not the choices we make every day regarding regular life, such as to where to live, what to do, whom to marry, or what to have for breakfast. It is about making the choice to embrace or reject the Love you are. It is about the choice to live in a way that sees and knows what we are behind the masks we wear. It is about becoming reacquainted with the original you that is witnessing your life.

I, like you, have worn many masks: son, brother, husband, friend, and professionally—paperboy, car detailer, grocery clerk, house painter, steam cleaner, EMT, cardiology technician, emergency-room technician, triage technician, recovery-room technician, aeromedical dispatcher, licensed aircraft dispatcher, tour guide, pharmacy technician, craniosacral therapist … writer.

Through all those different external roles, one part of me was always the same: the part that existed before this body did and will peacefully leave a little richer when this body has taken its final breath. With knowledge of this eternal part, the fear of death is erased; in fact all fear is erased. When one can *feel* the true nature of what one really is, the peace of God is inevitable. To this is what we must aspire.

The most liberating thing one can do is to release into life as it is, which means to transcend the smallness of the ego. And we do this by coming into experiential contact with the loving force which lies at the heart of creation. This force is within you right this very moment.

With this awareness, we learn we are inextricably connected to each other; we are in fact inseparable, and with this knowledge come tolerance, compassion, and a deep respect for others and their experience. Violence against others and ourselves becomes impossible.

When we accept our lives fully, with all of the mistakes and all the flaws, we open ourselves to health and joy beyond description, we reawaken into who we really are. We help others the most by simply elevating ourselves to a more loving place. The vibration will affect and transform those around us. There is no way it cannot. In fact, the best thing we can do for our society and our world is elevate ourselves back to our rightful place of unhindered, unrestrained, and fearless Love from which we came. The rest will follow.

It's time to let go of the friction and suspicion, to let go of the doubt, struggle, and pain. It is time to let go of the fight, the battles held within and without. It is time to let go of the reins held so tightly, the control cherished and held so closely. It is time to let go of all that is mistaken for safety but is in reality chains in disguise.

It's time to let go of all eagerness to judge and criticize, and all attempts to quantify life. It's time to let go of any need to defend what you think is right or wrong. Let go of all anger and hate. They do not nourish. They only degrade and destroy.

Slow down. Take a breath. Feel your heart beating in your chest and let the knowledge of that miracle lead you to an awareness of the sacred nature of you. Extrapolate this to all around you: the trees, the air, the water, the deer, the sun and moon—all of nature. What a gift you have been given. What perfection is held in your next breath! Realize every gnat is a miracle, as is every blade of grass. How often does a day pass that we are so busy with the menial tasks that we fail to see the glory of life?

The opportunity for loving peace is ever present, it is truly in every moment, and in fact, it is *only* in this moment. When found, don't let it go. Ego will attempt to distract you. Don't let go of what inspires you; don't let go of what energizes and enlivens you.

Give yourself permission to live; it is okay to be and express who you are. We so often don't, because we fear what others may think or we fear that being ourselves will somehow change the course of our lives, and it might. What is wrong with that? Is the course of your life set in stone? If it is, who did the setting?

It's okay to be who you are, it's okay to be happy, and it's okay to dream. It's okay to truly celebrate life. I'll give you permission, if you feel you need it.

The greatest discovery is that of finding out who you really are and then living *that* life. We are to live the path we are meant to live, even if others don't understand it or feel the need to criticize or judge. Know that when others feel that need, it is a reflection on them, not you.

Even when life is hard and full of struggle, even when we are in pain and suffering, all is ours. All is the way it needs to be for us to do what we are here to do, which is learn. *Period*.

As I write this several days before the supposed end of the world on 12/21/12, I am surrounded by fear. It is an interesting time and environment in which to write such a book. But this world has been defined by suffering for millennia; our spiritual evolution has been painfully slow. Within every moment and within every thought, there lies a choice of how you want you and your world to be. There lies a choice of what you want to teach, what you want to take with you when you leave this place.

Do you want to teach Love or fear?

Do we want a world defined by Love or fear?

What we want is to be free. We are meant to be free, we crave it, and we long for it. But free we are not when we are held within a prison created by our thoughts. Free we are not when we dwell endlessly on anything other than the moment. Free we are not when we criticize and judge every little thing in our experience. Free we are not when we regret the past and fear the future. Free we are not when part of us is screaming for us to touch upon the ecstasy of what lies within us right here and now. We have forgotten what the present moment feels like; it is foreign to us. Ironically, the present seems a million miles away while the illusion created by our memories of the past and the projections into the future seem real. We have spent enough time in the illusion; it is time to come home.

*Trust* is a big word.

Trust the nuance, trust the gut, trust the tears, and trust that flash of light you think you saw that passed so briefly, that you dismissed as not real. Trust those flashes of insight, those feelings that something is guiding you, that shiver up your spine. Trust those things; they are more real than you can imagine. They are the reality. This is the dream.

The secret to a joyful life is simple. Trust God, trust Love, and trust yourself.

The key to dispelling all fear is simple as well: know God is Love, know you are Love and then *trust that with all you are.*

With this knowledge, what is there to fear?

As I wander this beautiful planet, seeing, touching, tasting, and feeling my life, I am reminded of the contrast between where I have been and where I am. I have lived the suffering, I have lived the apathy, I have lived the darkness, but I have also lived the light. I know and have lived the contrast. I know both sides of the coin, and for this, I am eternally thankful. I know the glory and freedom of reemerging into what I truly am, of shrugging the false, and as I awaken, I thank my pain and suffering for leading the way back.

This world was created for you. It is a stage, and it is where you roam and interact with an environment perfectly designed for you to thrive for the purpose of reacquainting yourself with the true nature of existence, which is Love. Energy in, energy out. In an endless chain of divine expression, you experience your world and yourself in a perpetual dance, forever coming closer to the heart of creation or spinning away from truth. It is your choice.

CHAPTER 19

# *Epilogue*

I finished this book on December 14, 2012, in the late afternoon, Eastern Standard Time. I had been sequestered all that day and had not heard any news from the outside world until my wife came home, upset about something. I quickly became upset as well when she told me what had happened in Connecticut.

When I first heard it, I was sick to my stomach like everyone else. Twenty innocent angels mowed down in the prime of their trusting innocence, along with six adults. Why?

I was stunned, then angry, then sad. I thought of the message of the book I had just written, and I wondered, *Did it say enough?* And I knew I had to write a little more.

I have repeatedly said that our experience and knowledge of Love is gathered by our experiencing the horrors of what it is not. Well, we have once again seen the horrors of what it is not right before our eyes.

As I sit here on the sidelines, letting the politicians and media comment, fight, and speculate about the cause, I try to keep my own ego in check and not be offended by the reaction to this tragedy. However, I have to ask this: Why do we always seem to miss the point with such things? Why do we think we can legislate ourselves out of a moral or spiritual crisis? How is it that we think another law can or will actually change the way people behave?

For our society, this problem is packed with the potential for growth, and for that, we must thank the victims. They gave their lives for us to be given the opportunity to once again learn life's most important lesson. Will we honor them this time by actually doing so?

Mass shootings are a very difficult-to-ignore symptom of a society that is lost in every way. They are society's version of cancer; they show us where we are lacking Love in the most heinous and graphic way imaginable. And they are a warning.

It is shocking to know how many guns with which we are surrounded in this country, but it is even more disturbing to realize that there are this many people who are ready, willing, and able to coldly and methodically murder innocents. It is sobering that there are humans walking the earth, sharing the same air as the rest of us, who have come from the same Source as the rest of us, who have it in them to even contemplate—let alone perpetrate—the execution of children.

Do I wish we lived in a world without guns? Of course, I do. And I wish we lived in a world without a need for a military force, borders, police, laws, or nuclear and biological weapons.

Any sane person would wish for these things, but we don't live in that world. Due to the differences generated by the judgments of the ego, we do need some of these things, unfortunately. This is where we find ourselves as a species after many years of denying our own gifts and decency. Violent and divided is our present and self-imposed reality.

We are mad; our children entertain themselves (kill time?) by graphically killing people in video games and by going to movies rife with violence. We fear a child may see a woman's nipple during a movie more than we fear that same child seeing multiple people being shot to death in the latest thriller.

We are told by the experts this is a complex problem, which I believe is drivel and just further egoic nonsense. It is not complex. Love's lack is always the problem, and Love's acceptance is always the answer. There is no way in all of existence that someone who is not confused as to the nature of himself and his Source could ever, *in a billion years*, murder another human being, let alone a child. It is impossible; I cannot put it any more plainly than that.

The ego thinks it can think and solve its way out of anything, that for every question there is an answer. But the heart knows there is only one answer.

I can guarantee that many who read that statement will think it is small—naïve, perhaps. They will insist that we either need to get back to fearing God or that we need more gun control; they will insist we need studies and papers written by people with alphabets after their names to tell us what is wrong with us. They will insist that making Love, and by default what many call God, the reason and defining force of our lives is somehow insensitive to those who have their own beliefs.

Once again, it isn't complicated. There is Love and nothing else. If that sounds like a controversial statement to anyone, regardless of religious beliefs or lack thereof, well, then we are indeed lost. And things like this will continue to happen.

Make no mistake: fear is not of God; it is ours alone to bear.

I can tell you that as long as children are conceived in loveless unions, raised in loveless homes, and forced to live in a loveless world, things like this will continue to happen. When children are taught to fear and that they are finite, small, and vulnerable; when they are minimized and abused; when they are held from day one in a prison of limiting, painful, and fearful thought; things like this will continue to happen. Things like this will happen until we as a race finally learn.

This is the definition of a spiritual problem: one for which laws are not, nor could they ever be, the answer. I don't know about you, but it is not laws that keep me from killing someone. It is my inherent knowledge of the divine nature of my brother, it is my inherent respect for my fellow man, and it is a deep awareness of the essence and reason for life far beyond anything any politician could ever will or force me to do. I think this is true for most people, even if they don't know it.

And just like with everything else, we continue to mistake symptoms for cause. These shootings and all the violence we perpetrate against each other every day is a symptom of a completely confused, utterly lost, and frighteningly out of balance human race, one that lives without an awareness of its most essential and life-giving essence. And as always, it is much more effective to treat the real cause. The problem is that, due to their own propensity to suffer stunning mistakes of perception, those in power cannot even agree on what the cause actually is.

It is apparent that the more civilized we think we are, the less civil we become. We seem to define technology as the hallmark of our advancement, which is at the very least confused. I define our sanity by the relative compassion, understanding, and Love we extend to ourselves and others.

It saddens me to say we have a long way to go.

Made in the USA
San Bernardino, CA
09 May 2015